WHAT OTHERS ARE SAYING

"You don't have to be an elite athlete to understand the mindset for peak achievement. Darren is a master at translating those principles of preparation and execution to your financial performance to help you achieve all-star status and live your best life"
— **Harvey Mackay**
Author of New York Times #1 best seller
Swim with the Sharks Without being Eaten Alive

"Darren shows us how we can make our money work while we are out living life with those we love. He exposes our financial blind spots and proposes new daily habits to build a solid financial platform and live life in a financial "flow state." Darren's advice has helped me reorganize and recreate a much healthier financial flow."
— **Ian Lopatin**
cofounder of Spiritual Gangster

"Darren's knowledge and expertise about finances, getting my financial house organized, are amazing, but his white glove concierge-level services set him apart from the crowd. No one understands finance and treats their clients better than Darren Wright. Not only is Darren a trusted advisor but an expert at helping me achieve my goals, and he truly loves and cares about his clients, which is what's most important."
— **Dave Scatchard**
Fourteen-year NHL pro, international speaker, bestselling author
of *The Comeback: My Journey through Heaven and Hell*,
founder of Allstar Coaching

"Darren's advice and coaching feel like chatting with a childhood friend and a financial health expert in one. His ability to connect and simplify complex individual situations aligned with goals and the current economy is impressive, making him a prepper's dream for financial readiness. Darren greatly assisted this twenty-year Special Operations veteran, providing simple yet effective strategies for thriving on the financial battlefield and perspective on moving into and staying in financial flow."
— **Eric Ballester**
Special Forces, twenty-year USAF Combat Controller (retired), board member of Shields & Stripes

"It is rare to meet a person fully dedicated to financial wellbeing, the art of living and moving in wholehearted integrity. Smart, funny, and deeply human, Darren not only lives an artful life, he is aware that his purpose in life is to enable all of us to grow to live and love and serve others from flow consciousness. His book offers a way of living that enables our financial lives to align with our joy and purpose in life. With deep appreciation,"
— **Jeanne-Marie Mudd,**
Spiritual Wellness Advisor Canyon Ranch, Watershed Ways

"Darren is uniquely talented in helping people discover or rediscover what is important to them and get focused on the necessary mindset [one word] and action steps required to achieve important goals. As someone who started with nothing and built a very large, multistate [one word] and country international real estate company with thousands of employees, I recognize the value of delegation, coaching, support, integrity, and surrounding yourself with the right experts and leadership team. I consider Darren a skilled and trusted advisor, coach, and friend."
— **John Goodman**
Chairman Goodman Real Estate Company,
Founder Goodman Racing, philanthropist

Peak
Financial
Fitness

Peak Financial Fitness

Activate the proven strategies of elite athletes
to create a blueprint for success
in your life and finances.

Darren J. Wright

Special FREE Bonus Gift For You

To help You to achieve more success, there are
FREE BONUS RESOURCES for you at:
www.FreeGiftFromDarren.com

Podcast: "Finding Financial Flow," hosted by Darren Wright on Apple,
Spotify, YouTube, and other social media platforms.

Developmental Editing by Josh Iverson, Nathan Hassall, and Jen R. Miller
Cover Image by *Shutterstock*. Used with permission.
Cover Design by Justin Cook, Sprout Media

ISBN 9798392299430 (softback)
ISBN 9798391795445 (hardback)

Printed in the United States of America.

10 9 8 7 6 5 4 2 1

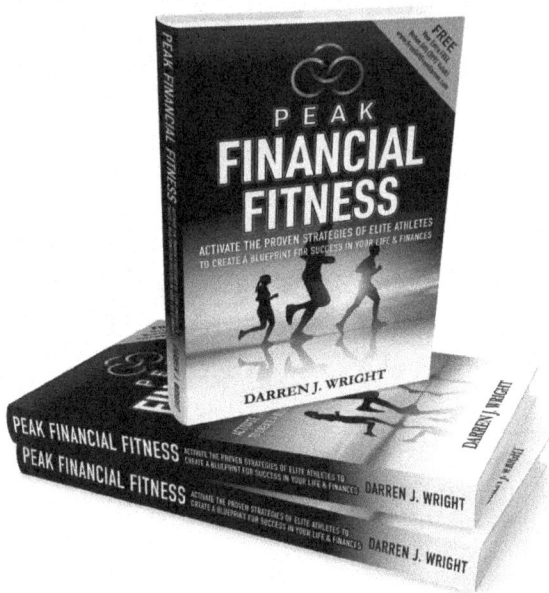

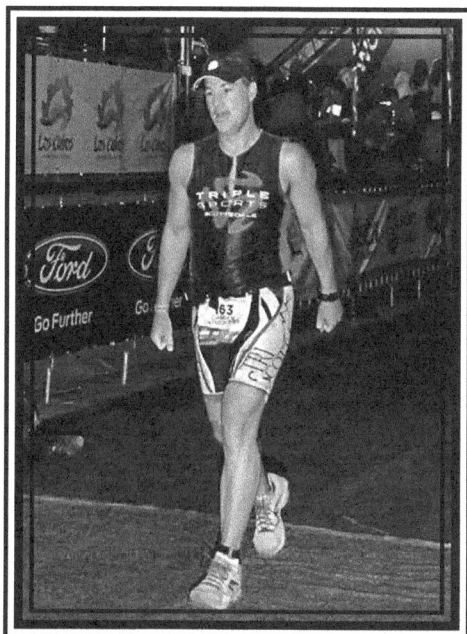

Contact or Schedule Darren to Speak:

The Financial Flow
480-268-5505
7135 Camelback Rd., Suite 230, Scottsdale, AZ 85251

Darren@TheFinancialFlow.com
www.TheFinancialFlow.com

Special FREE Bonus Gift For You

To help You to achieve more success, there are
FREE BONUS RESOURCES for you at:
www.FreeGiftFromDarren.com

Incredible FREE training inside!

DEDICATION

To each of our military members and first responders serving our great nation, holding the line on yeoman's work day in and out. As I wrap up this book, my son Cal is headed to boot camp, enlisted in the US Navy. May he and all the new, courageous enlistees of our armed services embrace the commitment to serve our great country.

To Pam, my beautiful wife, you're my rock, you keep me grounded. Without your love, friendship, and support over these twenty-seven years of marriage, I would not be the man I am today.

To my children Sam, Maddie, and Cal, you've taught me to be the best dad I can be and you've shown me how to love so deeply that my life changed for the better. Sam, I love your integrity; Maddie, your energy and the love you show to all; and Cal, your empathy.

To my mom, thank you for showing me the value of hard work and inspiring me with your years of tireless dedication in serving others.

It's not the strongest species that survive,
nor the most intelligent, but the most responsive to change.

— Leon C. Megginson (paraphrase, Darwin origin)

CONTENTS

FOREWORD

Peak Financial Fitness is far from your typical boring finance book. Darren Wright has written a comprehensive roadmap that compares the principles of achieving elite financial shape to the physical conditioning and routines of some of the world's greatest athletes. The examples are a great way to understand the visualization, imagination, organization, and discipline that fueled their successes and greatness, and the bonus is getting to learn many of the fascinating backstories of these world-class athletes.

Achieving peak financial fitness, like conquering elite physical fitness, presents us with a host of different strategies, advisors, and all sorts of people who are out to sell us all sorts of stuff that pads their pockets instead of our bank accounts. Even the best and brightest get sidetracked or swallowed by the variables—as you'll see in this guidebook to getting your financial house in top shape.

The benefits? Aside from building and protecting your wealth? Ongoing peace of mind and more free time to enjoy what you most love in life. Darren shows us that financial fitness is not just about us working harder, but how we can make our money work while we're out loving life with those we love.

Peak Financial Fitness is an important book, set apart from all other financial books by taking a holistic approach to building and managing your financial house—and your whole being and lifestyle. Darren's approach guides you to set up the life of your dreams and build a financial plan that supports your dreams and goals. He has laid out principles and practices that show how to persevere through challenges, to work with a financial head coach (trusted advisor), to produce a winning financial formula, and live an abundantly prosperous life.

The Result? Darren teaches us how to construct an elite financial house of strength, growth, and fortification that will not only move your money to work for you but withstand the worst of economic times.

I'm a believer, and am privileged to write this foreword because I, like many, have struggled to find good, clear, easy-to-follow financial advice to build my wealth and resources and set my family up with financial strength for future generations. Darren's advice has helped me reorganize and recreate a much healthier financial flow.

In this practical and actionable book, Darren exposes our financial blind spots and points us to daily habits that can lead us to achieve and live life in a financial "flow state." He analogizes this by the flow state elite athletes strive for and attain and the critical importance of a trusted head coach and team of specialists who help to shape and refine them into Olympians and champions.

Whether you're living paycheck-to-paycheck or have amassed a fortune, *Peak Financial Fitness* is for you—for everyone. Darren shares the reality of where most people are on the financial fitness scale. He motivates us to know ourselves better, map our dreams and goals, and to dig in and get going, move forward, and organize our financial lives while gaining clarification on the myriad financial options. The key is the mindset and support of your coach and trusted advisors to choose only the products that are the best fit for your individual desired lifestyle. This book shows us why optimal financial fitness cannot be achieved by following the one-size-fits-all plan.

A financial house of peak and fortified fitness begins with a trusted advisor and a custom blueprint drawn from your individually unique life goals and dreams, and how to build that elite financial house from the foundation up. This is how you make the most of your financial opportunities.

Your financial fitness is not only about how you most want to live your life today and all your tomorrows, but also about taking the best care of your loved ones and leaving a fortified financial legacy, so you will have more to share.

I hope you enjoy reading this book and that it will help you build a healthier you and a more prosperous future.

— Ian Lopatin,

Spiritual Gangster Cofounder

ACKNOWLEDGMENTS

Thank you to all the phenomenal coaches and teachers I've had in life. So much of who I am today is because of you.

Chris and Erica McClurg, thank you for introducing me to the triathlon sport, and for coaching me over the years in the sport, fitness, and life.

I will forever be grateful for the late, great Robert Kersting, Sr. for introducing me to the financial services profession and getting me started. Rest in peace.

Alex Vie, thank you for keeping our team engaged and focused on our mission as a financial advisory team, critical for our clients' overall success, keeping them on track to achieve all their important goals.

Bill Bachrach, thank you for introducing me to delivering a category of one business model and to raising the level of service, so high that anything less than exceeding someone's expectations falls short.

Thank you to my friend Jean Marie Mudd of Canyon Ranch.

Editors Josh Iverson, Nathan Hassall, and Jen R. Miller, thank you for your refining expertise in this book.

Dear Reader,

Thank you for investing and believing in yourself
toward entering fully into your unique financial flow.
This book is for you, designed to help you every step of the way.
Welcome to your new and improved financial future.

Warm regards,

Darren

PROLOGUE

All growth depends upon activity. Life is manifest only by action.
There is no development physically or intellectually
without effort, and effort means work.
—Calvin Coolidge

I was outside at 5:00 a.m. on the dark Kailua-Kona morning. I had arrived on Hawaii's Big Island on October 12, 2018 for the World Championship Ironman. For me—a financial expert in average physical shape, not a professional triathlete—the day was the realization of two dreams: taking part as a Kona Ironman and having the chance to cross the finish line in the greatest event offered in triathlon sport.

Elite pro athletes and amateurs had traveled from around the world. An annual pilgrimage to pay homage to the birthplace of the sport, and to test what we were made of in the grueling day ahead.

After hugging my family, I carried their good-luck wishes as I walked my bike onto Kailua Pier and into the Ironman transition area. Athletes, crowded in, were busy checking and double-checking their bikes and making final preparations to begin the morning's first leg: a 2.4-mile swim in Kailua Bay.

The air was heavy with athletes' nervous energy as we thought of the hot and brutal day ahead. I meet eyes with a couple of others, the air a thick rope between us. Slicing through the rising adrenaline tension was the overhead bladed chop of the NBC Sports helicopter, videoing the setup.

Praying for strength and reflecting on my training, I thought through everything I had accomplished to have the privilege of taking part in this race. The sea's lapping and sprays echoed my past coach's words: "When you feel those butterflies in the pit of your stomach, the trick is to visualize them all aligning in formation, headed in the same direction, and use that flow as a tool to propel yourself forward with total confidence."

So, I did.

2017 Ironman World Championship, Kona, Hawaii

I took on a mindset of steel determination and moved forward.

A comfortable calm I'd never forget draped me. At that moment, I knew anything was possible by working hard and believing in myself. From the depths of my heart, I was certain I was exactly where I was meant to be—time had slowed and I was completely present in the flow state. The butterflies had aligned with my body and mind. Nothing else would steal my focus that day.

An average athlete like me, competing in such an event, proved that peak performance in anything is available to everyone.

∾ *What you have to do and how you do it are incredibly simple. Are you willing to do it? That is another matter.[1]* — **Peter Drucker**

I started competing in triathlons twenty years before that Kona Ironman day. Each experience was varying distances, including sprint, Olympic, and half Ironman. Each event was progressively more enjoyable as my body became increasingly accustomed to the challenges and my mind learned I would always get to the finish line, one mile at a time. The experiences prepared me for Ironman—a 2.4-mile swim, 112-mile bike ride, and a 26.22-mile run, a total 140.6 miles.

When competing in an Ironman, there's the necessity to physically train for twenty-four months prior. The need to develop prime competing shape and prepare for anything and everything that can happen on race day. In any ten to twelve-hour event (swimming, biking, and running), there's the potential for mechanical problems and a host of other issues. Such challenges like nature's elements, gastrointestinal issues, cramping, and fatigue can affect performance.

∾ *Some people dream of success, while other people get up every morning and make it happen.* — **Unknown**

In various endurance races I competed in and also observed, there were challenges, like severe physical injury, that can take down the best athlete. Adversity will inevitably punch an athlete in the face. Thankfully, most challenges are minor and many are mental, requiring practiced mental strength. An athlete in a grounded mental flow prior to a race is more likely to handle adverse circumstances in advantageous ways and persevere to the finish.

During the 2014 Ironman in Cabo, Mexico, I experienced critical mechanical difficulty. Installed on the road and race course was a series of raised, one-and-half-inch square reflectors, about six inches apart, every ten yards. Hitting one while biking could flatten a tire. I had to focus energy on threading through those to avoid a mishap. But, sure enough, I hit one. *Fsssssssssssss.* A flat tire.

My bike had "run flat" tires, designed for the rider to inject air from an aerosol can that would keep the tire tube inflated for the rest of the race. Unfortunately, my run flats didn't work as advertised. Although I had inflated the tire, I wrestled with a continuous slow leak, constantly looking down at my rear tire, for the rest of the race, punched in the face by the distraction of having to monitor the tire closely to ensure the rim wasn't rubbing. I also had to stop periodically to inject more air and had to carry my bike to the next air station.

There came a point where my tire was so low that the rim was scraping the ground. I needed to find a quick solution. I slung my bike over my shoulder and ran down the main road in Cabo, searching for a station to refill the flat tire. The trek was hot and sweat poured down my face and body.

The worst thing? Being on foot, not once but twice, about a combined mile.

Frustration expanded my chest. Although every detail of a race is pre-planned and considers what could go wrong, carrying my bike for thirty minutes, looking for an air station, was defeating enough for a steel-willed athlete to consider quitting. My game plan was completely thrown off.

For long endurance races, planning also includes getting a nutrition regiment to a T. Everything's measured, down to the exact calorie, the electrolytes, salt, and carbs. Every hour of endurance training and racing, the body depletes around 300 to 400 calories. An endurance athlete will consume those precise calories across many hours and will limit water intake to an exact amount to avoid over-hydrating.

So, using energy wisely is a must, and neither do you want to underdo it.

When punched in the face—like having to carry a bike for thirty minutes—you feel messed up physically and mentally from a planning and training perspective. And to make matters worse, the Cabo race promoters ran out of water on the bike course and resorted to handing out clear plastic bags of water.

At one point, I pulled into an aid station and found twelve athletes without water. As ridiculous as the next tidbit sounds, adding insult to injury, the aid station attendant was nowhere in sight and found napping behind the tent. Yep, during the race!

After riding another grueling three miles, I eventually neared the finish stretch where a friend—elite athlete Erica McClurg (a participant) told me I was going the wrong way.

What?!

Frustrated but determined, I turned around, knocked out the miles I'd missed, and finished the race properly.

Why did I turn around when I could have continued on, nobody the wiser that I'd shaved off a few miles? Because I would have known. Integrity, taking the full challenge to finish was important to me. Although the total race distance was 140.6 miles, my distance turned out to be 142.6!

 ~ **Life isn't about avoiding obstacles; it's about how you handle them.**

The perfect test for my values was Cabo Ironman.

As obstacles appear, and no matter how much you plan for those, life can and often will upset the plans. The key is to be prepared for the unexpected, be willing to change plans, be ready to improvise as needed, and be steel-willed to reach your goals, no matter what.

As frustrating and demanding as the Cabo race day was in part, I still enjoyed the challenge and crossed the finish line, and although I was tired, I felt grateful.

Once I moved across that finish line, I plopped into a baby pool of ice, soothing for my aching muscles. Then I grabbed a slice of pizza and a cold beer, hugged Erica for her accomplishment (and she hugged me for mine), hugged my buddy Chris and my wife, Pam.

Unlike Cabo, the Kona Ironman course was smooth for me from start to finish, but prior, I faced a major challenge.

To take part in the hallowed race, potential participants must either qualify with a world-class time or gain pledges for charity, at least $40,000, during the race year.

I was raising three kids, coaching their sports, doing a fair amount of community volunteer work, and running a busy financial firm. This was not the time in my life to train for an elite competitive time to qualify. So the alternative was to raise pledges for charity.

My friend Chris McClurg knew my dream to compete in the world championship, Kona. He heard that Arizona US Senator Kyrsten Sinema had a charity slot available through a charity she was involved with, and he put me in touch with her. I needed to raise $40K within three to four months. I raised $45K and entered Ironman Hawaii. I was grateful for the spot she made available to me to represent a worthy cause, Women for Tri.

By the time I found a charity to represent, I had only four months remaining to train for the race. In perspective, a minimum of eighteen to twenty months of dedicated training is required to get an athlete's body in proper shape to take on an Ironman. I wasn't in great shape—certainly not Ironman ready. I was twenty pounds overweight, having not been in serious training for eighteen months. But the race was important to me, so I set out to do what I needed to do.

The key to getting my body in the best shape possible within a short period was enlisting accomplished triathletes who helped me from a training and nutrition perspective, as well as laying out every step I needed to follow to finish the race.

Based on my fitness level, I had no illusions about setting a personal record. My goal was simply to finish the race.

In the end, competing in the Hawaii Ironman was a transcendent experience despite, or maybe because of, the challenges: a limited training window and getting out in the community to raise qualifying charitable funds for entry.

Yes, it took a lot of work to make my dream a reality, but the race location, the team of people who helped me prepare, and the event combined generated a personal peak performance experience.

> *We cannot start over, but we can begin now, and make a new ending.*[2]
— **James R. Sherman**

As we'll explore together in *Peak Financial Fitness*, managing your finances offers similar challenges. A fact of life is that things don't always go as planned. Timelines can be out of your control and setbacks are likely to occur, making you question why and what you're doing, who you are, what you want from life, and more.

Throughout this book are stories of elite athletes and coaches who personify the proven principles, practices, strategies, and steps I teach to help people achieve peak financial fitness and their life goals. You can get your financial house in elite shape and overcome challenges, much like an athlete on the road to greatness.

To reach your peak financial flow, you must have a well-designed plan and, preferably, a great financial team, or at least the steel-will and determination to self-improve your financial knowledge and abilities, and push through setback and the redundancy of the grind, grit, and resolve that's necessary to achieve peak financial fitness that produces more free time and peace of mind to pursue and achieve your biggest dreams while enjoying the smaller joys you cherish.

Peak Financial Fitness will walk you through the breakdown of three key elements to achieve optimal financial fitness: planning, hard work, and expertise. Optimally, your plan will include a trusted financial advisor overseeing a team of financial specialists (for example, insurance, taxes, and investments). I didn't complete and finish Ironman competitions on my own. I realized the wisdom of enlisting the help of a seasoned team who knew all the ins and outs and ups and downs of athletic achievement and were equipped and experienced at seeing the end goal and laying out all the specifics needed to achieve that goal while holding me accountable, helping me through the steps and setbacks, and celebrating with me the wins.

Ensuring your financial house is in peak fitness is much like the steps taken to build a quality physical house: acquire a trusted, professional architect and contractor who brings in and oversees all the construction experts, like foundation setters, builders, drywall installers, electricians, and plumbers.

Experiences shared in this book highlight the fact that the principles of elite athletes also work for average athletes and apply to the financial fitness and success of both the ultra-wealthy and those who have modest bank accounts. While the stories of elite athletes and billionaires may seem more spectacular and attention-grabbing than the average person, the *principles* underlying their success can turn average into elite, across the board. It's the principles that matter.

The fundamental point is this: you don't have to be the best athlete and money manager in the world, nor in a certain sport or financial arena to succeed or enjoy an activity and lifestyle. But if you want to be the best you can be—at anything, including your finances—there are certain approaches, principles, patterns, practices, strategies, steps, and tools that lead to that success.

Peak Financial Fitness also includes many techniques that apply to anyone of any financial means who's interested or determined in getting their financial house in peak fitness and maintaining that fitness. The result is greater peace of mind and more time to enjoy the individuals and activities you most love. For example, I enjoy a weekly hike for fitness, inspiration, camaraderie with family and friends, and for meditation when alone. My home region,

Scottsdale, Arizona, provides many hiking opportunities.

On a hike of Camelback Mountain with a friend, we discussed how great it was to regularly step out of the rat race to focus on other things that mattered to us, and to gain perspective. Achieving a financially fit house will also allow you the funds to enjoy other experiences that reap deep rewards. Even if you're simply interested in building wealth, or you're green in financial matters and want to grow and start building wealth, investing in retreats and hiking experiences, for example, can help you leap forward toward reaching any and every goal and dream you want to reach in your life and the legacy you want to leave.

I'm just an ordinary guy who enjoys athletics, pushing myself, getting better, and optimizing and challenging myself to my limit. But competing in and finishing an Ironman is proof that any ordinary person with a desire can climb to the top of their game, including financially. I wasn't the top Ironman finisher in Mexico or Hawaii, but I had top commitment to be my best as an athlete—for myself. Using principles that apply to athleticism can help you become and maintain your best financially: peak financial fitness.

Good timber does not grow with ease: the stronger the wind, the stronger the trees.[3] — **J William Marriot**

INTRODUCTION

There is nothing worse than doing the wrong thing well.
If you want something new, you have to stop doing something old.
— Peter Drucker

Focusing on your endgame—the aim of all your hard work—will help inspire you to reach your goals. Likewise, *Peak Financial Fitness* will also help you enter fully into your financial flow—your financial house in elite fitness, organization, maintaining those, and attaining your life desires, more freedom, greater peace of mind, security, and joy.

But why "elite" financially fitness?

Personal finances are indelibly tied to every aspect of our lives. Achieving and maintaining optimal financial fitness will help to ground you, not just financially but mentally, emotionally, and practically. Pursuing peak financial fitness will draw you into self-reflection to understand what's important to you personally about money and specifically define for you your life desires and goals, which then enable you to flow more freely, in a financial flow and every other area of your life.

Your freer mind and freed up time will enable you to enjoy more of your life and pursue activities you love or want to explore apart from work and earning money. Perhaps your desire is more peace and freedom to write a book or a blog, explore other careers or business goals, focus more on your relationships, take more vacations, have broader travel experiences, practice art, hike—anything that will deepen your self-reflection and heighten your joy.

How much do you think Steve Jobs would have paid at his death from his multi-billion-dollar fortune to buy back his normal life expectancy?

All of it.

Peak Financial Fitness answers why an organized, team-based approach to financial management, led by a trusted advisor, is essential to improve your financial fitness: helping you align your choices with your most closely-held values and important goals which lead to getting your financial house in peak shape.

If you decide to take the lone route to manage your finances, this book offers you essential facts and tools you can apply.

Peak Physical Fitness Mirrors Peak Financial Fitness

Rewarding and fulfilling to me as a veteran financial professional since 1993 is helping my clients achieve their important goals, move closer to their financial flow, and thrive in life. I'm grateful to have met so many wonderful, inspiring high achievers of zest and grit and helped them achieve their important, individually unique goals, living a purposed life. Fascinating, successful, high-net-worth families, business owners, NFL head coaches, professional athletes, entertainers, and CEOs of some of the largest private and public companies. The natural next step was to offer you fundamental financial education and tools in book form, to help you protect and grow your money and achieve the life you most desire.

Throughout this book, I often cite pro athletes who illustrate the principles underlying success. For instance, I've long admired and been a fan of Jack Nicklaus, 6 Masters wins, 18 major championship wins, and 73 PGA Tour victories. He was aptly nicknamed The Golden Bear.[4] We can glean much about financial fitness from the examples of pro athletes demonstrating the principles of success.

While raising his family, he also became an accomplished designer of golf courses—because he wanted to. Impressive. He designed the two courses at Superstition Mountain Golf & Country Club, forty-five minutes East of Scottsdale, Arizona, and the results were spectacular. The course Prospector was completed in 1998 and Lost Gold was completed in 1999.

In the late 90s, while Jack was using his artistry to finish his vision for Prospector, I toured the raw site, all dirt and sand, with Jack and Lyle Anderson, a golf legend dubbed "the father of desert golf." Afterward, along with Jack's wife, Barbara, his son Jackie, and a few others, we had dinner. I was privileged to listen to Jack, The Golden Bear, describe in more detail his design vision for his masterpiece. Hearing him describe his vision was a moment I will not forget.

Jack had taken a wise route. He stayed organized, and he delegated tasks to a vetted team, which allowed him the freedom to focus on his unique skill sets as a pro golfer and designer. Delegation to experts was key to Jack's freedom and peace of mind to pursue his love for golf as a career and design golf courses—his passion became his business!

If I were to ask you what job you would most like to be employed in, you'd likely share your passion—your dream job. Our dreams are achievable when our financial houses are in peak financial fitness.

Teamwork was essential in Jack's family life as well. In his interview with *Elite Traveler* (2018), he said, "For the first 45 years of our marriage, my wife was my main support team."[5] He described how Barbara's management of their home (her desire) allowed him to focus on taking care of business on the course. The result of delegating and teamwork was Jack's freedom to focus on and amass the highest total Grand Slam wins in history. He's considered a golf legend and icon, one of the greatest golfers of all time.

Jack said, "To have the ability to balance work and family, to not let the business end dominate, and to take care of the most important things in your life, that is the most gratifying feeling ever."[6]

FINANCIAL MANAGEMENT APPROACHES

Over the years, I've witnessed various approaches to helping people with their financial planning and organization. While some approaches are more successful than others, I've discovered that beyond applied techniques is the conceptualization of the strategy.

It's one thing to take a specific approach to managing your finances and another to understand the philosophy behind the approach.

> ⟿ *In this world you're either growing or you're dying, so get in motion and grow.*[7] —**Lou Holtz**

This distinction is important because, as I've observed, the people who best understand the logic behind their approach are best able to implement and stick to that strategy. This insight became important as I contemplated writing this book and otherwise sharing my knowledge of the financial planning process. I place emphasis on a holistic approach to optimize the probability of achieving financial goals. A key component is knowing and articulating your values. *Forbes* Expert Panel wrote:

> Some people know and can clearly state the values they hold dear. For others, however, articulating their values isn't so easy. Coming up with a

clear and coherent set of personal values can feel overwhelming; getting guidance on how to work through the process can be helpful.[8]

Understanding your values is crucial because your values give you clarity in decision-making.

When I set out to write *Peak Financial Fitness*, I asked myself, *What's the best way to convey the principles and practices underlying holistic financial planning, incorporating a values-based approach?*

After much contemplation, the answer hit me: *Elite athletes practice many of the same fundamental principles of holistic financial planning.*

So, as this book's tagline reveals, I use sports anecdotes, metaphors, and parallels to explore how elite athletes achieve greatness, peak fitness, and maintain their performance. The financial parallels to athleticism provide a simple means for driving home powerful truths. I'm not inferring that financial planning (holistic or otherwise) is simple. However, given that the topic can be complex, analogies based on sports can provide a powerful means to better understand the principles of holistic financial planning.

One such principle, as I've mentioned and we'll explore deeper in Chapter Three, is entering the "flow state." Some people refer to this informally as being 'in the zone.'"[9] We lose track of time as though effortlessly flowing.

Achieving the flow state proffers better outcomes and our actions feel effortless.

Like athletes experience "the zone," it's possible for us to experience a flow state when working with our finances. Not just in selecting and dealing with financial matters, but letting your finances work for you so you can undertake activities that allow you to experience flow.

If peak financial fitness is analogous to peak physical fitness, what exactly is peak physical fitness? Being in the best physical condition you can achieve—not as compared to others. Likewise, elite financial fitness is individualistic, not defined by being better at finances than other people. As often said in sports and the arts:

⁓ **At the end of the day, the race is really with yourself.**

Fitness means getting the most out of your unique ability, to compete against yourself to achieve your best self.

Elite physical fitness centers on maximizing your unique ability. You may perform a sport at your peak ability only to find that others are better. The first fact is that you are not "others." Perhaps they had better training, a better coach, or they're naturally more physically gifted—faster, stronger, or a better build for the particular sport. What others have doesn't matter, physically or financially. Your only competition is yourself.

Comparing yourself to someone who has more money isn't going to help you get your financial house in elite shape that aligns with your particular values. You may manage your finances well yet have a lower net worth or net return than others. In both cases, the point is to focus on what you can control and what works best for you.

Once you've done what it takes to reach your peak financial performance and you're maintaining that flow, you've positioned yourself to reap the rewards. *Peak Financial Fitness* examples show how to get yourself in peak condition financially and physically.

Through the pages of this book, I'll cover the fundamentals of holistic financial planning for you to achieve and maintain elite financial fitness as demonstrated by the concepts of peak physical fitness. I will guide you through this flow state model as though you're one of my clients and help you move fluidly along in your financial journey.

⤳ Desire is the key to motivation, but it's determination and commitment to an unrelenting pursuit of your goal—a commitment to excellence—that will enable you to attain the success you seek.[10]
— **Mario Andretti**

ATTITUDE: THE KEY TO ATHLETIC AND FINANCIAL SUCCESS

Attitude is a powerful component of success. Whether your aim is athletic, financial, business, relationships, or anything else, your attitude plays a large part in determining your results.

Foremost, you need to think BIG! Big goals, big dreams, big life.

Consider elite athletes and top-ranking teams. Their big dreams helped to fuel their rise, and many took big risks, as you'll see later in this book. But taking a similar approach to your finances does not mean you must take big risks; it means aiming for the stars. If you only reach the moon, you'll have achieved higher than if you'd simply aimed to reach the treetops.

～ Where you are today is based on where your mindset was yesterday.

What is your mindset toward money and managing your finances?

Consider the steps needed to develop a professional or elite athlete as compared to developing a well-cut and shining diamond. A raw diamond is formed over time and under great pressure, and in the hands of an expert diamond cutter, the gem becomes a wonder to behold.

The best athletes are those who begin with the determined mindset that they have potential. They grow under the pressure of that determined attitude and relentless practice, and in the hands of their coach and support team of experts (nutritionist and various trainers) they refine their flow state and become a lasting wonder, like legends Jack Niklaus and Mario Andretti and the others I mention in this book.

With a determined attitude and effort, financial knowledge can grow in us from the books we read, financially focused people we meet, and the financial experiences we encounter in daily life. But our knowledge can become refined by teachers, mentors, and coaches, taking us to the next level of financial fitness.

The initial challenge is that much of the written advice and teachings are for the masses rather than high achievers who endeavor to reach big goals and dreams. There's not a one size fits all when it comes to advice. What works for someone who's just getting started in wealth-building doesn't necessarily work for someone who's very wealthy. This book, however, is for everyone: those who are building wealth via savings and investing, those who have a lot of wealth, those who have little, and for anyone who desires to begin the wealth-building and financial fitness journey.

Whether you think you know a lot or a little about managing your finances and making money work for you as opposed to you working for money, *Peak Financial Fitness* is for you.

Regarding those who have a lot of money, I'd wager to say that 99.9 percent believe they don't need to know more because they think they have all the answers—until disaster strikes. We'll look at those examples as well.

First, consider your mindset.

⌒ The soul becomes dyed with the color of its thoughts.[11]
— **Marcus Aurelius**

Having a lot of money is often equated with a financial house that's in peak shape. This attitude is hubris and a serious mistake. There are plenty of examples—wealthy sports stars who, upon retiring with millions in the bank, squander it all and end up declaring bankruptcy. They may have had a lot of money, but they lacked what's most important: adequate financial planning and management.

You may have $20 million and your financial house may be fine, relative to spending. However, we can't ignore the repeating demonstration of wealthy individuals declaring bankruptcy.

I've had conversations with world famous athletes, distressed by their grave financial losses. They came to me for guidance to reconstruct their financial houses on the foundation of solid principles and strategies. Becoming financially fit also rewarded them with peace of mind and a greater flow to enjoy the things they loved most.

Even more rare (like red diamonds) are the wealthy who have such large balance sheets or net worths that financial challenges are less likely to hit them.

⌒ **Caution: never become arrogant about your finances and loss risks.**

There are plenty of recent and historic examples of the very wealthy losing tens of millions of dollars because they thought (like most) that money made them bulletproof and that due diligence was too big a bother. Not so.

You may remember, or may have been one of the approximate 37,000 people among 136 countries who collectively lost $65 billion[12] because of Bernie Madoff's Ponzi scheme. The late Madoff started as a Wall Street investment advisor in the early 1960s as a penny-stock broker[13] but wasn't registered as an advisor until 2006.[14] Eventually, he gave many investors promises of ridiculously high returns on their investments—classic Ponzi scheme stuff. Strangely, he was already unbelievably wealthy, yet he engaged in fraud. Classic greed over grateful.

While people were handing their money to Madoff, thinking they would get a consistent return on their investments, Madoff was using their funds to pay for his lavish lifestyle, investing his clients' money into his personal bank account.

The returns Madoff paid to initial investors were the money of other investors. In 2008, when some investors requested to cash out, to the sum of around $7 billion,[15] Madoff couldn't pay up, and the house of cards started to crumble. Plenty of wealthy people lost millions, including high-profile people like Kevin Bacon, John Malkovich, and Larry King.[16]

Ultimately, the spawn of Madoff's greed was his wife leaving him, a son's suicide, and losing his own life to a prison cell under a sentence of 150 years.[17] He died in prison, disgraced.

There's also FTX, a crypto-trading company founded by Sam Bankman-Fried. On the wings of hype and some excellent marketing, FTX's worth rose to $32 billion.[18] Major firms invested in his company to the tune of billions. However, although money was flowing into the company, not much was flowing back to investors. Many newspapers, including The Wall Street Journal, stated that FTX had to pay out $8 billion[19] more than the company had. Many investors lost their money, including Tom Brady, Larry David, David Ortis, and Kim Kardashian. Anyone who had as little as $1,000 in crypto lost money.

Dramatically, in just one fateful week, Sam Bankman-Fried's net worth— which had raised to $16 billion—vanished to zero. Nothing left.

The most recent Ponzi (2018) exposed schemers Jeff and Paulette Carpoff, owners of DC Solar, who with their growing ring of greedy thugs smooth-talked their way into stealing a collective billion dollars over the course of nearly a decade that even "hooked Warren Buffett and the U.S. Treasury!"[20] The US transportation secretary chose DC Solar, "as a partner in the Obama administration's Smart City Challenge, which pressed cities to adopt climate-friendly technology."[21]

While the DC Solar scam targeted major corporations, this travesty is essential to mention for two key reasons.

1. The scheme cost tax payers. US Attorney for the Eastern District of California, Phillip A. Talbert, stated, "Jeff Carpoff orchestrated the largest criminal fraud scheme in the history of the Eastern District of California, ...costing the American taxpayer hundreds of millions in tax credits."[22]

2. You may be a business owner or other executive, considering investing company funds in a trend. Don't simply trust smooth-talkers and

investors, nor halfway pursue proof of product. Take due diligence seriously. Use due diligence checklists, making this essential task a part of your grind on your way to the top and to ensure your longevity toward reaching the top, safely legal.

As we see, regardless of wealth level, there are consequences for not having our financial houses in elite shape. You may cruise along for years with no negative financial issues, but time will probably catch up to you and catch you off-guard, unfocused, not living in alignment and in your authentic financial flow.

Ask yourself this: *Do I want to be financially successful and have the assurance that my financial house is in peak fitness and protected, or do I want to gamble the risk that my financial house will magically remain in perfect order?*

Simply put, can we expect our physical homes to remain pristine and solid with little to no attention?

To choose peak financial fitness means choosing a better life—more confidence, peace, free time, with a greater ability to get what you most want from life. To choose otherwise is unthinkable, right? There are consequences for every action and inaction and can lead your financial foundation to crack and crumble beneath your feet because it wasn't properly laid and maintained.

∼ Peak financial fitness applies across the wealth spectrum.

An individual without substantial wealth can build a financially fit house to withstand the most powerful financial storms and achieve their financial goals—just as the person with average athletic ability can develop their physique and skills to be their unique best in their recreational sport.

A person with tremendous wealth may find that getting in top financial shape is necessary to hold their current financial position or make the most of their financial fortune.

∼ Peak financial fitness means having your entire financial house in perfect order.

Ask yourself this question: *On a scale of 1 to 10, where am I in terms of my financial house being in perfect order?* One being total disaster and ten being the perfect role model we all should follow.

Where are you on the scale? Most people don't know. Through my many years in finance, my experience is that people, on average, rate themselves at 7 or 8, some at 9. I've met people with significant wealth whose financial health was actually hovering around a 3 or 4.

Wherever you'd place yourself on the scale of financial fitness, compare that rating to the photo below. The single house still standing examples what a 10 looks like in a financial disaster, with everyone else at a 6 or 7.

The owner of that physical house had done what it takes to build a solid foundation, erect a stellar framework, and apply fortifying finishes. They began by consulting with experts to ensure their house would stand the test of time and disasters and maintain peak results.

Aftermath of Hurricane Ike, 2008, home of Warren and Pam Adams[23]
Photo by pilot Ray Asgar, Smiley N. Pool/©Houston Chronicle. Used with permission.

You can imagine what the many neighbors may have told the homeowner during construction and throughout maintenance. "You're being extreme! Overly cautious. There's nothing wrong with being a 6 or 7," they may have added. "Besides, it's too much work to become a 10 and stay at that peak. What's the worst that can happen?"

In my experience, people rate themselves highly when they're actually at 5 or 6 on the financial fitness scale. Most don't know where they actually stand and their answer is a gut reaction based on their perceived financial expertise. This is interesting because when I mentioned "getting your financial house in order," most people hadn't heard of this.

As my friend Harvey Mackay told me,

~ *Don't accept mediocrity and never lower your standards.*

Even if you have what you think is a ton of wealth, bad things can happen. A payment takes you by surprise, emergency medical dramatically alters your life and medical bills hit you, a risky investment doesn't pay off, you overpay and spend too much on things you don't need, and your bank account plummets. Many people live paycheck to paycheck. Do you know how many? Here's a frightening statistic, even more when you consider the risks life brings: As of this writing, 60 percent of American adults—including over four out of ten who are earning high-income—live paycheck to paycheck.[24]

If you want to take a comprehensive, holistic, fortifying approach to managing your finances, you'll find this book helpful. *Peak Financial Fitness* covers a broad range of financial planning concepts that will be useful to every adult with wealth or not:

> Those who are financially successful or have some financial success and are looking for approaches and strategies to help them manage their finances and achieve the next level, tailored to their goal.

> Those with less financial success who want a guide to a healthier financial house.

> Those who can only guess where they are on the financial fitness scale and those who believe they know but haven't taken the proper steps to learn the reality of their financial fitness.

Instead of zeroing in on a particular investment strategy, product, or budgeting method, *Peak Financial Fitness* focuses on overall holistic financial planning—getting your whole financial house in peak shape rather than focusing on repairing or renovating a particular financial aspect and discarding the others.

Taking a comprehensive approach to your financial affairs implies much more than basic planning. While there may be the rare individual who can successfully manage everything—career, family, social life, and optimal financial fitness—such an individual (in my experience) is truly rare.

Your financial fitness provides and protects the most important aspects of life's truest wealth: your family, your peace of mind, and your discretionary time.

TRUE WEALTH IS DISCRETIONARY TIME!

Time is a priceless factor. A financially fit house provides more time to focus on non-delegable things like family, physical fitness, mindfulness, hobbies, and other pursuits of happiness.

~ Financial management is a delegable task.

The same fact applies to the world of competitive sports. Occasionally you find a self-taught golf pro like Bubba Watson—twelve PGA Tour wins with two Masters, an Olympic appearance six national championship appearances[25], and peaked at second place in the world.[26] Watson is very much the rare exception, having no formal lessons. Most professional athletes had extensive coaching on their way to the top and continued seeking guidance from coaches after reaching their pinnacles.

⁓ If we command our wealth, we shall be rich and free; if our wealth commands us, we are poor indeed. — **Edmund Burke**[27]

Thinking in terms of the team-based financial approach and how you can set that up, consider the following mental exercise to help you gauge the fitness of your financial house:

> ➤ Tell me about the quarterly meeting you have with all your financial technicians gathered in the same room on your behalf. Is everyone knowledgeable and aligned as a team regarding what's most important to you about money and your specific current and future goals and dreams, and is everyone working together to achieve those?

> ➤ Have you ever experienced such a meeting, dedicated to your unique and best interest—no conflicts of interest?

> ➤ Who would run that meeting if you were to arrange it?

> ➤ Would you know all the questions to ask?

We can conceptualize such meetings by drawing from Nick Saban's football coaching style resulting in seven NCAA National Championships—the first with Louisiana State University and six more with the University of Alabama.[28]

Saban is legendary for his play after play video-watching that gave him detailed knowledge of each player's strengths and weaknesses. He incorporated that knowledge and focused dedication into every detail of practice. His flow expertise helped him work out what was best for each athlete and kept each player on track to hone their unique strengths and improve their weaknesses. Saban gave his athletes the best advice and tactics for their individual athletic and team success, and ensured the implementation of his guidance and strategies by enlisting a team of coaches who focused on differing areas of success. The results of his focused leadership over the coaching staff and athletes were multiple national titles.

How great would it be for each of us to have a Saban in our lives, strategizing our financial fitness with microscopic focus and flow that ensures the success of our individual goals?

But financial meetings?

If you're like most people, you probably haven't enjoyed the various financial meetings with your independent tax, legal, insurance, and investment technicians. Such meetings typically feel like a "gotta do," like visiting the dentist. Perhaps location convenience draws you—meetings with your string of professionals independently by Zoom or over coffee or lunch. Although the settings may be convenient, such meetings are not optimal and not necessarily what's best for your elite financial fitness.

A trusted advisor will do what is best for your financial welfare rather than what's convenient. This means your advisor will

> schedule detail-focused meetings with you,

> have no conflicts of interest,

> use state-of-the-art technology,

> offer access to knowledgeable, vetted, and experienced experts in their respective fields, and

> offer the best agenda for each meeting.

Another example mirroring the purpose of a trusted advisor is a general contractor overseeing the building details of your custom home to ensure everything is well-attended to, quality, and timely. Would you just hand him a list of your desires and say, "Call me when the house is built?" Or would you meet with the contractor on a regular basis and watch the construction and the care taken as progress unfolds?

Your financial meeting agenda should involve the best processes and methods—truly holistic— including:

> account reviews,

> detailing every type of insurance you're carrying and whether you still need those policies, and making sure the needed policies are up to date at all times,

> reviewing your taxes to insure total accuracy,

> making sure all legal matters are up to date,

> keeping you on track to achieve your unique goals,

- delivering the most appropriate advice, and

- exploring vetted investment money managers that are most appropriate for your unique goals.

While taking this detailed, focused team approach may seem logical, such a reality is uncommon for most folks. They take a fragmented approach to their finances—purchasing a financial product here, getting advice about retirement there, buying insurance elsewhere, and so on.

Consider this truth: your financial fitness is fundamental to everything you do and desire in life and affects every aspect of your life. Taking a fragmented approach to such a critical life foundation is suboptimal.

The financial fitness principles and strategies in this book are key to you gaining more discretionary time, monetary growth, financial stability, and peace of mind. While the planning and process may feel a bit inconvenient, the rewards are worth it.

In my role as a trusted advisor and team leader for a group of high-achieving, goal-oriented families, I tell them, "Achieving peak financial fitness isn't about what's convenient for me or you; it's about doing what's best for you to optimize and maximize your specific goals."

My role in financial fitness, like Saban's role to his coaching staff and players, is focused on creating the best experience tailored for you to:

- help you achieve your goals,

- in alignment with your most closely held values, and

- facilitating what's most important to you and your family, no matter what.

What does such a crucial experience look like? I hold meetings in my office where I can create an optimal experience for each client. The phones are turned off to avoid distractions, there's optimal lighting in a relaxed setting, the financial information I share is well-prepared, tailored to the client's values, and clearly communicated. The meetings are recorded to preserve the dignity of every detail and to ensure no detail is missed.

How would you answer these vital questions:

- On your calendar, do you have scheduled with your advisor an annual cycle of quarterly financial meetings?

- Is each meeting focused on each differing element of your financial plan toward your highest probability of financial success?

- Do you feel that being a laser-focused financial athlete at those meetings is a good use of your time?

- Regardless of your financial circumstance, do you want to be financially fit? I believe you do since you're reading this book.

Perhaps you have millions in the bank and you either want to safeguard your wealth or grow it. Or maybe you have a modest account and want to create a plan to help you live within your means or build your wealth or both.

A well-designed, properly organized client progress meeting will take sixty minutes of your time for an annual total of about three or four hours. This is the time needed for you to stay on financial track.

My firm's meetings with our client families are organized and facilitated like board meetings. Between meetings, our subject matter experts (team members) execute their respective specialty in alignment with the family's expressed goals. Reporting is in simple terms, using simple reports and language that paints the full picture for the family and helps to ensure the client is staying on track with their financial goals. When a client is off track, we inform them and provide the strategy they need to follow to get back on track.

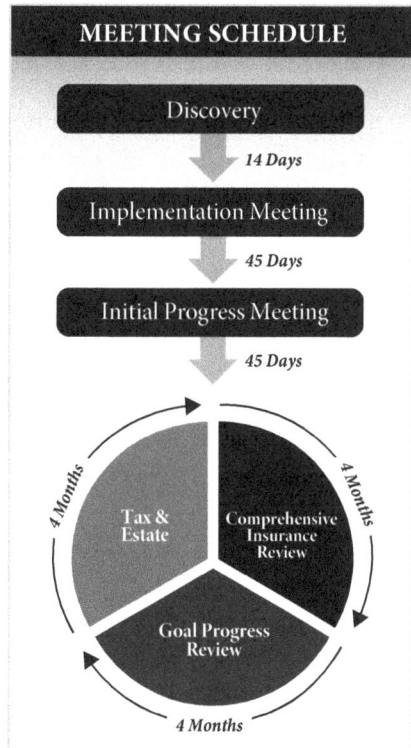

MEETING SCHEDULE

Discovery

14 Days

Implementation Meeting

45 Days

Initial Progress Meeting

45 Days

4 Months

4 Months

Tax & Estate

Comprehensive Insurance Review

Goal Progress Review

4 Months

Do you experience this level of focused help with your financial house?

Perhaps you're wealthy and feel you don't need such assistance or improvement. Here's the caution: ego tells us we're in control of our finances when we may not be and when we slip and lose control.

Maybe you're not wealthy but you think there's nothing that can improve your financial house. And perhaps your mindset is: *This is my lot in life.*

That thinking is also ego speaking and what's keeping you on a hamster wheel, repeating the same route, not advancing financially toward your desires. Maybe you're aware that you're stuck but don't know how to exit the wheel. This book will show you how to free yourself.

You may be the rare exception: your financial house is in peak shape and you're reaching all your current goals. Despite that, it's likely you could do even better with a team of experts guided by a trusted advisor with your interest at heart.

    ~ **The key ingredient to managing finances well is to put ego aside, pursue the wisest path, let go of the outcome, and trust the process.**

I didn't write *Peak Financial Fitness* merely to help you improve on what you're already doing. If that was the case, I wouldn't be raising the bar high enough for you, since I know there's so much more advantage available to you. Therefore, this book is about steering you away from suboptimal financial management and into your greatest level of financial health.

In short, should you desire complete, holistic financial fitness, I encourage you to assume the role of chairman over your finances and to enlist a trusted adviser as your personal CEO.

CHAPTER ONE
Getting Your Financial House in Peak Shape

The way to get started is to quit talking and begin doing.
— Walt Disney

Wildly successful tennis pros Venus and Serena Williams had to devote time, focus, and determination to achieve peak physical and mental shape to excel at the greatest tennis height. From a young age, their father, Richard, dedicated his time, focus, and determination in coaching them while their mom, Oracene, played a key supporting role to help them achieve their aim.

The sisters have shared incredible success in tennis and in the sporting world at large. Especially impressive was their unorthodox path that began in Compton, California, a South Los Angeles city that was unfairly represented by gang violence at the time.[29]

The girls broke the mold of expectations for how tennis players looked and acted and the results were historic. Venus's first professional game was in 1994 at age fourteen. Serena followed the next year at age fourteen.

Both continued to excel on a steady and sturdy path despite setbacks, like their parents' divorce in 2002 and Venus's 2011 diagnosis with Sjogren's syndrome, an autoimmune disorder.

At this writing, the sisters have been in the game for over two decades. Together, they've achieved thirty grand slams, including fourteen for women's doubles, and three Olympic gold medals.[30]

The uniqueness of their story is that the girls are sisters who both became superstar tennis pros, and neither at the expense of the other. They shared healthy competition, played each other in the finals of various tournaments, won championships on the same team and doubles, and each had times of victory over the other. Serena and Venus are examples of committed excellence to the best of their individual abilities—not competing against each other but bettering themselves as individuals.

Once the family moved to Palm Beach, world-renowned tennis coach Rick

Macci saw the sisters' play and saw their extreme determination and desire. In a 2021 interview, Macci recalled the conversation he'd had with Richard that day. "'You got the next female Michael Jordan on your hand.' And [Richard] put his arm around me and he said, 'No, brother man, I got the next two.'"[31]

Macci was a tough coach and tough on himself because he wanted peak results. Even at this writing, Macci (age 69) gets up at 3:30 a.m., seven days a week, and puts in ten-hour coaching days.[32]

On Richard choosing him as a coach, Macci said: "Richard asked me 50 questions. If he was going to let someone in this circle, he wanted a role model, a father figure, a mentor."[33]

At ages seventeen and sixteen respectively, Venus and Serena met on a court at the 1998 Australian Open for their first professional game as opponents. The next year, they won the doubles event and at the US Open, Serena won her first Grand Slam singles title. They've both won many titles and played multiple finals against each other at Wimbledon.

ESPN cited Serena as saying, "Luck has nothing to do with it, because I have spent many, many hours, countless hours, on the court working for my one moment in time, not knowing when it would come."[34] Venus, equally poignant, told CNN, "I don't focus on what I'm up against. I focus on my goals and I try to ignore the rest."[35]

Like Saban, the sisters' focus was not on end results but on their individual goals, personal behaviors, and what they could control. They achieved getting their minds and bodies in a flow state that led to peak athletic success.

The same applies to getting your financial house in shape, focusing on your goals, your behaviors, and what you can control.

But what does it mean to get your financial house in shape? It's similar to getting your residential home in shape. You clean up everything, organize all your belongings, ensure that everything in your home is well-functioning (no flickering lightbulbs, no plumbing issues), and you have professionals in place to take care of issues and give you sound advice. For optimal value, you consistently make needed repairs to your home and upgrades when you have the means. The same logic applies to your financial house. But what about the repairs and optimizations needed that you're unaware of? Such concerns are among the reasons why having a professional, trusted advisor is essential.

Whether you live in the financial equivalent of a one-bedroom apartment or a ten-bedroom mansion, you can and should get your financial house in elite shape and maintain that peak fitness.

Whether your overall financial aim is simply to enjoy a nice outing once a month, take your family on vacation, or achieve total financial freedom, you'll understand the following by the end of this chapter:

- ▸ The problem with taking an uncoordinated approach to your finances.
- ▸ How your financial structure and professionals can work for you.
- ▸ Where you are on the 1-10 financial fitness scale.
- ▸ How to view your financial house from a holistic angle.

Should you get help to manage your finances? The short answer is yes, with an added "however." Our financial houses typically have several distinctive rooms—taxes, insurance, and investments, for example—and there's an overseeing financial technician for each. While you need such financial technicians (specialists in their respective areas of finance), the problem preventing peak financial fitness is lack of head coach for team management. Using the three examples above, do your accountant, multiple insurance representatives, and investment managers come together with you to help you create, carry out, and manage the best financial plan for your particular needs and desires?

I've met plenty of people who manage their personal finances the way they think they should, meeting individually with their independent financial technicians. The client may also have an estate attorney who drafted their trust documents, and their various independently operating investment advisors are likely competing for the client's returns.

Perhaps the individual has purchased a large life insurance policy or a few policies over the years for survivor income or estate tax purposes, but those independent technicians do very little if any teamwork between them for the client's optimal benefit.

I've also met many people who handle everything themselves, even their investments, which are typically unsuccessful or far from the success they could have if working with a trusted advisor who's coordinating and overseeing the technicians.

The point is, individuals without a trusted advisor, pulling together and overseeing the best and needed financial technicians, their financial houses are messier than they think, their money is not working optimally for them, and they may be losing money.

A critical problem that frequently arises when entrusting your finances to a variety of uncoordinated financial technicians is that those professionals are giving uncoordinated *advice*, treating your differing financial aspects as separate threads instead of woven together as the master tapestry representing your financial house. When operating individually, with no shared and collective goal with you, they're not able to weave those threads into peak financial fitness.

While specific advice may prove appropriate for an investment, contract, or policy, rarely are these needs properly coordinated and strategized from every possible angle. The result is a financial house that doesn't fully align with your values and overall objectives—the things in life that are most important to you. Uncoordinated financial management based on the individual function is generally suboptimal and counterproductive to those core objectives.

This common, fragmented approach is called "silo." Consider this approach from a sports angle. If Venus and Serena didn't have their coach, sports psychologist, fitness trainer, and nutritionist working together as a coordinated team with the agreed upon goal, the Williams sisters would not have fully excelled on the tennis court. Likewise, if an athlete is doing loads of strength training and their nutritionist is unaware, the athlete may not be maximizing the calories and protein needed to guarantee that their diet aligns with their training regime.

Even if you're working solo on your finances, it's wise to take the steps to be certain that all your financial documents are well-organized, each are working in line with your goals, and you're disciplined to stay on target to reach your goals.

Let's say you want to put an extra $100 per week into savings for a special trip abroad. Every Saturday evening, you go to the bar and spend $50 on drinks and another $50 on food. Compounding the issue, these lifestyle habits are causing your weight gain, and on Sunday, you feel too tired to do what's needed for your physical health and reviewing your financial fitness. You've lost the $100 intended for savings, lost a day to a pounding hangover headache, and your financial house remains in disarray.

If saving $100 each week is as important to you as a weekly night out and your physical fitness, a solution would be to go out once every two weeks, have one drink, and decide against the curly fries.

If you think saving $100 a week is enough to achieve your goals, but you aren't investing it where it can grow, that's not pursuing elite financial shape. You're simply doing better than you were and you may feel that your financial house is stronger, but that's not pursing optimal financial fitness.

Returning to the question, "Should I get help with managing my finances?" Financial Technicians are often focused on their specialty rather than your overall financial picture. The financial products featured for you may not align with your short term or long-term goals. This is not a dig at experts who provide specialized financial advice, but simply a warning that they don't often coordinate with your other technicians to pursue an overarching strategy for your elite financial fitness.

When considering the vibrant life you desire and the changing tax laws, investment rules, interest rates, variable returns, personal spending, and all else—importantly your goals, needs, and desires—there's a difference between a financial technician providing a product or piece of advice versus how that product or advice will affect your goals and financial fitness. Technicians aren't typically looking at how their advised product, strategy, and your circumstances may change over time, but offer you products and advice based on their best guess for your financial future. After you've purchased the product, the technician is likely less involved in your financial fitness because their initial work is complete.

Have you found that to be true in your circumstance?

Despite spending time and money to achieve our financial goals and prevent financial risks, most people's financial fitness, at best, is a 7 out of 10.

Whether an individual has a lot of money or a little, without a head coach (trusted advisor) overseeing the individual's (family's) multiple, independent advisors are likely lower on the financial fitness scale than they think. What does this silo approach mean consequentially? (1) Higher risk of financial loss when life hits them unexpectedly with a major challenge, (2) not reaching goals, (3) lifestyle suffers, which (4) affects emotional, mental, and physical health and spousal, family relationships.

Optimal is to manage your finances with a "holistic" approach: collaborative financial planning and management with professional oversight.

If your financial fitness is at a 7 or less, there are many common mistakes preventing you from achieving a 10 out of 10. A 10 does not mean billionaire status; a 10 means peak financial fitness regardless of your assets. The holistic approach is about improving and maximizing your unique situation and goals on the financial fitness scale, not about getting rich quickly or comparing yourself to others. The focus should be about what's uniquely best for you.

> ~ **The holistic approach to financial planning and management is a tailored approach that aligns with your particular needs and desires.**

Common mistakes people make when working with financial technicians include:

> ‣ assets not properly allocated to benefit from tax offsets,

> ‣ inefficiencies,

> ‣ too much or too little insurance or the wrong insurance,

> ‣ excessively aggressive or conservative asset allocation,

> ‣ inaccuracies in taxes or missed deductions, and lack of coordination of

all the different financial instruments in your tool box.

These problems are pervasive because silo financial management cannot ensure financial success. After all, advice given in a silo system is separate threads.

Let's do a mental exercise. Think of a microbiologist alone in the lab, looking into a microscope, both eyes pressed against the ocular lens, zeroed in on a petri dish. Rather than the ability to see what's happening in the lab, the biologist can only see what's happening under the microscope. Someone could quietly enter the lab, taking the biologist off guard, resulting in a destroyed specimen when he jumps and the petri dish takes flight, or can even steal from the lab without the biologist's discovery until after the fact. Why? Because there were no other eyes watching and protecting the bigger picture.

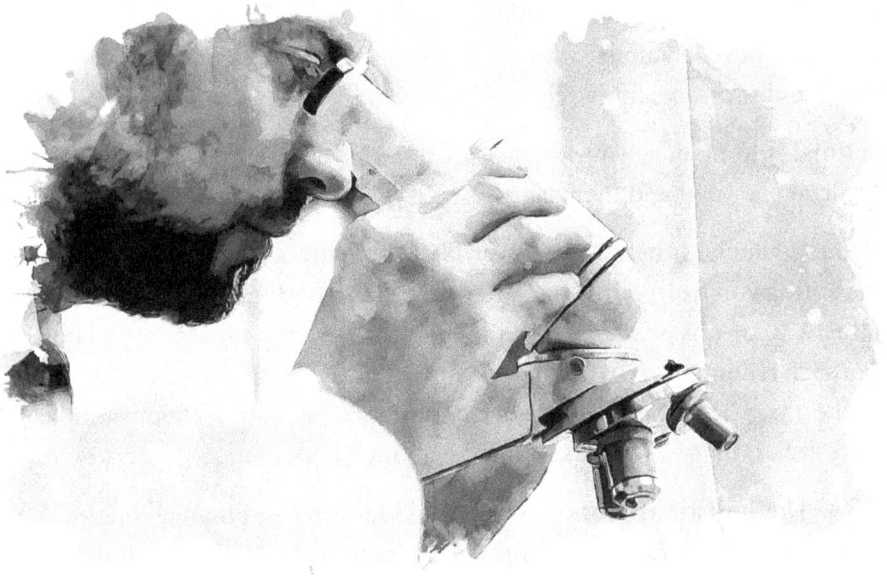

With that metaphor in mind, wealth performance at its best will have a shared oversight, maintaining watch on every aspect of your financial life, applying a tailored plan, and maintaining that unique, elite whole-fitness plan.

For this synthesis to be possible, you must also include realistic financial goals. An unrealistic goal, for example, is expecting your $10K to grow into

$1M by next week.

∿ Have big goals with realistic steps in a holistic financial strategy.

What is the goal of accumulating wealth? The answer is subjective to each individual.

Your answer might be, "My goal is to have enough money to achieve all my financial goals, have financial peace of mind, and more freedom to focus on my other goals. "

Someone else may say, "My goal is to challenge myself to be my best with my finances and to push myself beyond what I think are financial limitations— my aim is a billion by retirement."

Whatever your goals and financial management choice, when you achieve optimal financial fitness and you're moving in a financial flow, maintaining the best possible financial shape, you'll know and feel the success of overcoming obstacles, the satisfaction of having more time to spend in the most desired areas of your life, and you'll more fully enjoy your life. Perhaps you want more time to spend with family and friends or return to your hobbies and other personal goals. Or maybe you long to have more free time to practice your culinary skills, more time to exercise, read, travel, or write a book. And maybe you want to take up tennis or Ironman!

No matter your current level of wealth, achieving and maintaining peak financial fitness is about doing your best with the assets you have.

Like an elite athlete in training and competing, you must muster all your inner and financial resources (a collaborative team of experts) and be determined and disciplined in order to perform at your peak financial level, your money working for you rather you working for your money. The focus will not be about competing financially against others, but focused on what's uniquely best for you and your family.

My Ironman competing wouldn't have made sense if I'd competed with the sole mindset to win rather than doing all I could to compete with myself, doing my optimal best to push myself beyond my conceived limitations.

Shouldn't we have the same mindset toward our financial management, achieving our personal best regardless of respective net worth? I challenge you to set a lofty goal with a collaborative team of financial experts and achieve your objectives.

Again, aim big with realistic goals!

Let's say your personal goal was to finish a marathon in the top 10 percent of the event's racers, but you fall short, finishing in the top 20 percent. If you had aimed for the top 50 percent (a more realistic goal), the outcome would have been that you achieved higher!

~ **Lofty goals produce lofty results.**

Attaining the highest personal financial level is absolutely possible but requires dedicated time and work, like preparing yourself physically for the Tour de France, an Ironman, or reaching the Wimbledon finals. Achieving peak financial fitness is not out of your reach, nor is that goal and accomplishment restricted to a select few. You can achieve anything you set your heart and mind to.

Overcoming the factors preventing you from achieving optimal financial fitness means putting yourself in a position to maximize your finances and without regard to other people's wealth. What matters is what you have and how best to maximize your financial circumstance to achieve your greatest financial goals.

THE PLAYER-COACH APPROACH TO FINANCIAL MANAGEMENT

~ *Think of yourself as dead. You have lived your life.*
Now, take what's left and live it properly.[36] — **Marcus Aurelius**

As I've touched on, achieving peak financial fitness often requires letting others take the field. For instance, rather than you trying to pick investments, you're often better off hiring a trusted investment manager. The same goes for preparing your taxes, selecting insurance policies, and planning your estate, etc.

On the flip side, we know this scenario isn't always possible (at least for a season), which is okay and understandable—but going it alone is not recommended because you won't have vetted, knowledgeable experts to help you. Most important is having a trusted advisor at the helm to serve as the team leader.

If you must go solo for a time, also use that time to gain solid financial knowledge, strategies, and principles—as you are by reading this book—and stay prepared for financial obstacles and protected against risks.

This solo approach is like one of the most famous player-coach scenarios, when NBA legend Bill Russell served (for a time) as both the playing athlete and the coach, a dual role that's rarely seen in professional sports but sometimes deemed necessary. Russell was the all-star center for the Boston Celtics in the 1960s and both coached and played during his last three years on the team. The Celtics won NBA titles in 1968 and 1969.

While the complexity of sports today (at this writing) leaves the player-coach challenge in a past era—as with today's financial complexities—Russell's impressive run proves that this dual role can be successful with the right knowledge, strategy, and determination to work hard and achieve.

A more recent example is Lleyton Hewitt, Grand Slam tennis winner who served as coach and occasional player on the Australian Davis Cup team. Hewitt was a successful singles' player in his heyday, but in a pinch he played doubles for the Davis Cup team and did an incredible job.

In the financial player-coach role, reaching your peak financial fitness will be more complicated technically and time wise, but can be achieved.

There are three categories of people managing their finances:

> Do-It-Yourselfer

> Collaborator

> Delegator

Here are the pros and cons of each approach:

> **Do-It-Yourselfer**—You're the coach and player of your financial house. You're solely responsible for doing the detailed financial research and planning, making the complex decisions, weighing the risks, devoting your time to financial maintenance, and determining when you need to perform a financial task and when to hire a financial professional.

Managing your finances alone can work if you know what you're doing and can work to the best of your ability when you don't yet have the means to hire a trusted advisor.

Perhaps managing your money is your passion and you're working toward your financial flow state. If this is the case, you can become more adept at doing it yourself by training to become a certified financial planner.

If you're solo managing your financial house out of necessity, you can gain insight from financial books (thank you for reading this one!), from online information and classes, and by talking with financially fit family members and friends. The difficulty in this case is the unwanted weight and responsibility. Likely, you'd rather share the load with a trained and trusted team of professionals. If this describes you, consider whether you're open to tapping into the power of delegating at least some of your financial management.

> **Collaborator**—You're handling your finances but you consult with different professionals regarding taxes, investments, insurance, etc., either to deepen your knowledge, gain advice, or unload from your shoulders a bit of the time, weight, and responsibility. Regardless, the collaborator is similar to the do-it-yourselfer, not truly delegating nor leveraging their time. Much of what you learn as a collaborator you implement on your own.

Perhaps you view your financial professional as a mentor or as a gauge to see if your research aligns with theirs. Whatever the case, make sure the advice and information you're receiving is from a trusted financial advisor.

> **Delegator**—You prefer that your trusted advisor and coordinated team manage your financial house. You allow them to do that and you follow their advice. You allow them to do the research, and even though that option is available, you prefer to use that time to focus on what you most enjoy and what you want to achieve in other areas of your life, supported by the results of peak financial fitness.

My experience is that delegators get the best results in finance and other areas of their lives. They understand the *division of labor* law that applies and this wisdom:

⁓ **Surround yourself with people who are smarter than you.**

As you move through this book, consider these questions:

> Which category best describes your financial management?

- What reasons underlie your choice?

- How has your decision shaped your current financial fitness?

- How will your decision serve you moving forward?

If you have the means to hire a trusted advisor but you're a do-it-yourselfer, ask yourself why you would serve as the CEO of one of the most valuable and critical aspects of life? If you were running a corporation and it was time to grow, and you needed to sit as the board chairperson, you would either

1. hire a CEO to direct the day-to-day operation—someone who will do the job better than you or

2. continue to do the job but put yourself in the best possible position to ensure your finances will take the company as far as possible.

Let's say you have successfully achieved a 7 out of 10 with your personal finances and you're worth millions. Bravo! Now put intelligence and logic to work over emotion and consider finding a trusted expert advisor to take you to even higher levels. If you're not at this stage yet, this can be one of your goals.

The same applies in professional sports; solo-sport athletes and team sport owners hire coaches, trainers, and other experts to help them reach peak fitness and performance.

In my experience, there are wealthy people who are very knowledgeable about what made them wealthy, but like all of us, *they don't know what they don't know.* Wealthy do-it-yourselfers may think they're doing a good job managing their wealth, but they have nothing to measure their financial skills against. Some may only know how many digits are in their accounts. If this is you, you're at high risk.

To gain maximum benefit from this book—whether wealthy or of average net worth—I implore you to be open to becoming a delegator, whether that means now if you have the means. If not, work toward that using the knowledge you're gaining. Your life will improve tenfold. Delegating is the only sure way to reach a 10 out of 10 on the financial fitness scale.

Maybe you're already a delegator, following the lead of your financial advisor.

If so, consider these critical questions:

> Is your advisor a proven expert, capable of handling every aspect of your financial planning and management?

> Is your advisor a solo professional or overseeing a team dedicated to your best interests?

> If your advisor is solo, do you have confidence you'll achieve elite financial fitness—a 10 out of 10?

Prior to this book, were you aware of this concept—getting your financial house in 10/10 shape and order? If not, consider that none of your current technicians have brought this essential plan to your attention nor have acted to help you get your finances in 10/10 fitness.

> Is your advisor performing each of the following and more?

- Has asked all the pertinent questions to understanding your financial needs and goals

- Has implemented and manages a financial plan that aligns with your particular values and goals

- Advises you, meets with you regularly, and keeps you informed

- Reviews and chooses the most appropriate investments for your needs and goals, growing your money

- Is properly protecting and allocating your assets

- Has determined the insurances that best meet your needs and goals at this stage in your life

- Has ensured that the policies are properly set up for each of your trusts, various trustees, and beneficiaries

- Has provided advice on all other aspects of your financial house without the incentive of resulting compensation

TEAM IMPORTANCE

Think of pro football and all the various positions of expertise needed to create a formidable team that can make it to the playoffs and ultimately the Super Bowl. Now think of the team's lineman. What if the lineman was alone—no teammates—facing the opposing team and all the various obstacles alone. No quarterback, no running back, no fullback, no tight end, no wide receiver.

Will the single player make it to the Super Bowl? Will he make it to playoffs? Will he even win a game?

Becoming an expert in any of the various financial fields (like investments, taxes, and insurance) is difficult. And given how often financial laws and regulations change, and the volatility of the markets, maintaining that expertise can require significant effort. For example, reviewing and choosing investments.

A one-man band isn't capable of the achievement of a carefully orchestrated symphony. The same applies to you or a single financial expert toward achieving peak financial fitness.

Cautions:

In psychology is the Dunning-Kruger effect, coined by research psychologists David Dunning and Justin Kruger. The term refers to someone who elevates their ability or expertise beyond their actual skill level. For example, the lineman playing every team role, or a Division III quarterback thinking his skills are NFL level. In contrast to this effect, what's striking is that many people with true, proven expertise feel more doubtful and humble about themselves. We see this humility and the opposite—the Dunninng-Kruger effect—across the board in sports, music, and other fields, including finance.

Another psychological quirk is overestimating your skills when you experience a successful financial outcome (like an investment). We've seen this overconfidence in team sports; a winning team falling hard once they reach the playoffs. Likewise, when you have a financial loss, you may underplay that as "bad luck" rather than lack of expertise. The quirk is in thinking of yourself as a pro when you're not. The alternative is ensuring you have a truly trustworthy, expert financial advisor and team with a proven record of success.

Countless investment advisors will gladly take your money and charge you a fee to manage it, and sometimes that is the only path workable for you. It's the rare advisor who takes a flat fee to ensure no conflicts of interest, truly having your back.

If you think you're a finance expert and you're not—or you see signs that indicate your financial advisor is not up to par—your finances could be in a heap of trouble.

Those who have taken the time, energy, and dedication to study, learn, and practice a role or specialization are best positioned to succeed.

IT's UP TO YOU

Can you imagine someone saying they want to become a skilled tennis player but not picking up a racket and practicing? Similarly, if the person gets on the court and consistently tries to play but ignores the professional's pointers, will the player become better?

I can't tell you how many times people have told me, "I want to become more educated about financial planning," but took no action toward that goal, no matter what I recommended. This common scenario reminds me of someone who repeatedly complains, "I don't like my job," yet continues in the same position or with the same company.

As the adage rings true, the definition of insanity is repeating the same thing over and over and expecting different results.

Like anything in life, it's completely up to you how you manage your finances. While there are financial experts trained and seasoned to help, they can only help those who are willing to learn, ask questions, and implement the advice. Why take the time to expand your financial knowledge if you don't intend to put that knowledge to use?

Yes, putting in the time and work to become great at something is difficult. But those who truly want better results will put the work in.

~ The crux: do you truly want your financial house to be in peak shape?

If you honestly want peak financial fitness, you must act on that rather than merely hoping your financial house will magically thrive and maintain itself and hoping it will withstand the test of time and torrents.

Making excuses and not taking the steps to achieve optimal financial fitness is the easy but dangerous way to live. People who make excuses never reach peak financial fitness or any other desire that's littered with excuses.

~ Those who learn what they need to do and carry out are successful.

If you want a strong and lasting financial home, you gotta put in the work—even when that means sitting down with your collaborating team of financial experts for an hour every calendar quarter and applying their advice (or allowing them to apply their expertise on your behalf).

Here are three primary reasons people don't reach their goals:

> - the information or time dedication (or both) feel overwhelming

> - the information is difficult to understand and apply

> - lack of interest in the subject

If you fall into any of those categories but truly want your financial house to be in peak shape, a dedicated financial advisor can teach you, advise you, motivate you, and help you stay on track.

Again, whether your net worth is $100 thousand or $100 million, simply reading this book or others is not enough to protect or grow your assets, much less attain peak financial fitness. You have to do the work.

~ *Money is in some respects like a fire; it is a very excellent servant but a terrible master.* — P.T. Barnum[37]

⌒ Some people want it to happen, some wish it would happen, others make it happen.[38] — **Michael Jordan**

Just as an elite athlete began with a plan, you need a plan if you want to improve your financial fitness. The holistic approach is best because it considers you as a whole person—your hopes, dreams, life circumstances, beliefs, and goals—rather than simply considering your financial assets.

When you think about your finances from a holistic angle, you'll need to take these steps:

1. Identify what's important to you about your money. The answer should be unique to you.

2. Identify each of your tangible goals and, if applicable, your spouse's tangible goals.

3. Put those values and goals in writing, which will help you accomplish them. Why? Because writing creates motivation and accountability, which help us change our behaviors. By writing your values and goals, you're more likely to action that will help you achieve your goals.

4. Take full account of where you are now in moving toward your goals. This assessment will give you an even better understanding of what is required to achieve your goals.

5. Make a priority goal to hire a team of professionals to create a custom, step-by-step plan for hitting all your goals, staying on track, and otherwise boosting the likelihood that your plans and dreams will play out the way you want.

Any other approach is suboptimal, like this example: A potential pro golfer was an amazing collegiate golfer by his God-given gifts and skills. The prediction was that he'd become a stud on the PGA tour. Although he initially scored well and made the tour, he didn't hire a coach and he didn't further grow and strengthen his skills. He thought that relying on his experiences would be enough. He thought he was at a 10 at the sport, but he was actually at 7, and he had the mindset that reflected a 4.

It quickly became clear to everyone, except the player, that he would not make the PGA cut. He had been arrogant and thought his work was done.

The golfer didn't have a coach to help get his mindset right and toughen his ability to handle the pressure.

Lack of proper financial management is similar. The chances are greater that your investments will choke, you'll sell when you need to stay the course, and turn paper losses into real losses.

You may have built a large net worth, think life is easy and feel like Superman when times are good and the market is growing, but that mindset, my friend, is one of complacency and ego.[39]

No Rosy Period Lasts Forever.

The Dow Jones Industrial Average (DJIA) grew from 10,500 in 2010 to 35,908 in 2021. Do you know what the DJIA was in 2000? 10,500. That's right, essentially no gain that decade, known as "the lost decade."

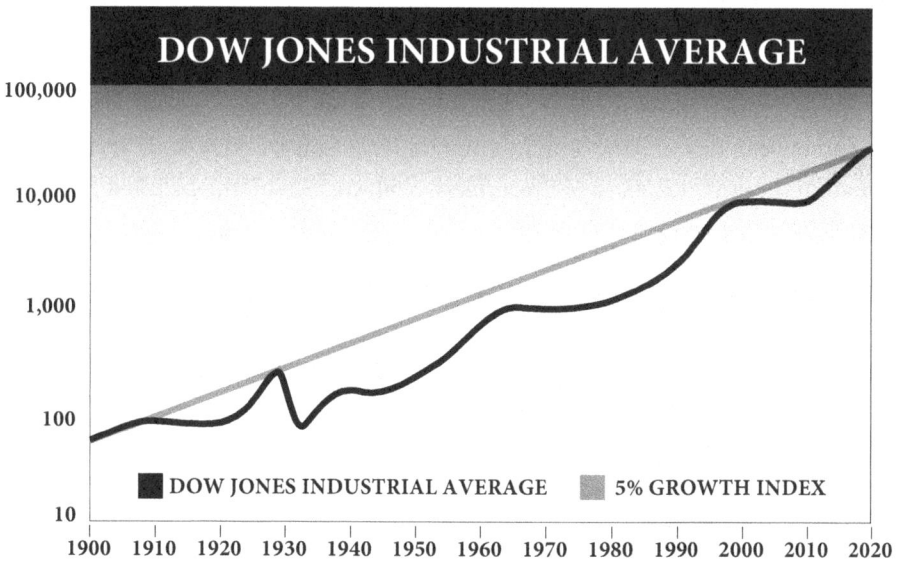

DOW JONES INDUSTRIAL AVERAGE

| | DOW JONES INDUSTRIAL AVERAGE | 5% GROWTH INDEX |

The Dow Jones Industrial Average (DJIA) is a price-weighted unmanaged stock index that measures the performance of 30 prominent companies listed on stock exchanges in the United States. It is one of the indexes used as a benchmark for other stock market indexes. Historical results include reinvested dividends, but not fees typically associated with investments (which would decrease performance). Past performance is not indicative of its future performance. Investors cannot invest directly in an index.

If you were investing back then, you knew that growing your investment and retirement accounts was harder. At this writing, the last eleven years have not been as difficult. But, what do the next ten years hold for you?

What if your net worth has grown and you have even more at risk? Example: You had $1 million in your retirement account before losing 9 percent, which took you down $90 thousand. You can recover from that if you're facing twenty more career years. But, if you just retired with $10 million and then lost 9 percent, you'd be down $900 thousand—a huge impact since you're now (due to the loss) deinvesting from a smaller pile of savings, and you can run out of money even faster.

Are you better prepared or are you winging it?

Do you have the experts in place to help you or do you have the same technicians who helped to get your financial house where it is today, perhaps a 6 out of 10 or less?

Don't you owe it to yourself to think outside of the box? To get better results? Peak results?

In the following chart, dating way back to 1900, you can see that the average return of the Dow Jones was 7.5% but the compounded return was only 5.3%. How was that possible? Money isn't math and math isn't money. For example, if you've saved $100K and put it in an investment account, and the following calendar year has a 50% return, your balance will be $150K. If in the next calendar year you have a -50% return, will your account balance revert to $100K? No. The worth would be $75K.

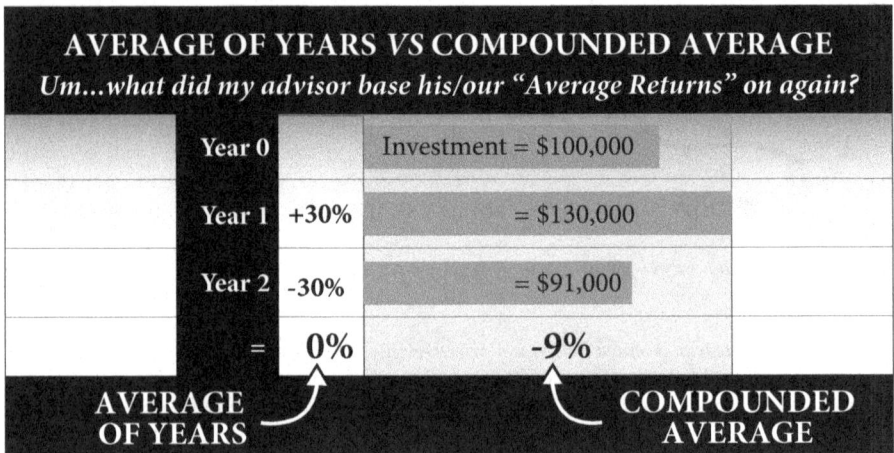

AVERAGE OF YEARS *VS* COMPOUNDED AVERAGE
Um...what did my advisor base his/our "Average Returns" on again?

Year 0		Investment = $100,000
Year 1	**+30%**	= $130,000
Year 2	**-30%**	= $91,000
=	**0%**	**-9%**
AVERAGE OF YEARS		**COMPOUNDED AVERAGE**

"Average Returns" don't always equal "Average Returns"

Wouldn't it make sense to just pay attention to the straight up returns or losses? You have to look at the actual dollar impact.

In the following chapters, we'll continue to explore the road to peak financial fitness and I'll answer this question: How can holistic financial planning best serve you?

Summary

> There's almost 100% guarantee that your finances are not at 10/10 on the financial fitness scale.

> Having lots of money doesn't mean you have great financial health and having less money doesn't mean you have poor financial health. We're competing to better ourselves.

> There's always more you can learn. If you get good advice from a trusted advisor, take it and put in the work.

CHAPTER TWO
Why a Holistic Approach to Finances?

I hated every minute of training, but I said,
'Don't quit. Suffer now and live the rest of your life as a champion.'
— Muhammad Ali

HOLISTIC APPROACH
TO SPORTS AND FINANCIAL MANAGEMENT

The most successful athletes and teams take a holistic approach to their sports. They don't boast of just ability, training, or fitness, they take a whole-view approach to excellence that combines optimal physical, mental, and emotional fitness.

This same holistic approach is mirrored in the personal finance management arena by individuals with financial teams of experts achieving the individual's and family's unique financial excellence in consideration of individual's and family's respective values and goals.

Legendary basketball coach Phil Jackson is the current Hall of Fame record holder for NBA championships and to date history's fastest coach to achieve 900 wins. Jackson was a countercultural icon of sorts by practicing the essential nature of the holistic approach in coaching, such as bridging Buddhist philosophy and Native American mysticism, which earned him the affectionate title "Zen Master."[40]

During his tenure as the Bulls' head coach, Jackson brought the determination to create team cohesion using the holistic approach that's also important in personal financial management. For example, he told Michael Jordan about the team, ". . . we've got to find a way to make everybody else better."[41] The result was six championships and at the height of his coaching awarded NBA Coach of the Year.

Regarding Jackson's holistic approach, he was known for the "one breath, one mind"[42] philosophy to team management, stating, "I approached it with mindfulness"[43]—a coaching approach that was comprehensive, the approach that's also most successful in financial management. Jackson said his approach wasn't just about physical strength from lifting, but also increasing mental strength through mindfulness. Even when something had gone wrong in the game as it will, like a bad call that benches a player, it's important for the player to recenter their thoughts, not on winning but on achieving one's unique best. The holistic philosophy helped Jackson's teams become successful. He said, "You have to get the spirit back into things."[44]

This mindset—a united team spirit—enables anyone to achieve peak financial fitness, success, and legacy within the individual's particular height of ability.

Kurt Rambis, former NBA player and assistant coach Jackson, explained Jackson's mindset, "He goes through an entire mental process of envisioning the season and how to get the team to the NBA Finals."[45]

In his book *Eleven Rings*, Coach Jackson wrote,

> The first thing I did with the Bulls was to teach the players . . .
> mindfulness meditation based on the Zen practice I'd been doing for
> years. . . . Though mindfulness meditation has its roots in Buddhism, it's
> an easily accessible technique for quieting the restless mind and focusing
> attention on whatever is happening in the present moment.[46]

Pro golfer Phil Mickelson's success depicts the underpinning holistic approach of mindfulness. At age fifty, Michelson became the oldest golfer to win a major championship. Given the bookies' odds of 1 in 300, Mickelson was clearly an outsider for the championship, though he'd won five previously. After his win, Mickelson said, "I've had a few breakthroughs on being able to stay more present, being able to stay more focused, and physically I'm striking it and playing as well as I ever have."[47] He had learned to calm his mind, which paid off for him at the 2021 PGA Championship.

Michelson's example, like many other high-achievers, proves that regardless of age or means, one can become financially fit and successful using the united team mindset of focus on achieving an individual's and family's values and goals.

In modern sports, holistic training is common to optimize an athlete's ability to compete because the holistic approach addresses the whole person. This approach often involves a detailed training regimen, nutrition, sleep regulation, fitness coaches, physical therapists, psychologists, and more. Athletes will use this whole-person training to achieve peak fitness in every regard.

Quarterback Tom Brady, twenty seasons with the New England Patriots and his final two with the Tampa Bay Buccaneers, retired as a legend at age forty-five with a record-setting career: the player with the most Super Bowl victories in NFL history. Brady, too, held a disciplined, holistic training regimen that included tactically mapping every aspect of his day, positioning him to train and compete at the highest level. In a post-game press conference, he said,

> . . . you can't go out and practice average on Wednesday and average on Thursday and okay on Friday and expect to come out on Sunday and expect to play good. If you practice great on Wednesday and great on Thursday and great on Friday, there is no reason why you wouldn't come out on Sunday and play great.[48]

The same principle applies to your financial planning and management. You can't spend one day a week making good financial decisions and the other six days treating your finances like confetti and expect to reach elite financial fitness. You won't.

Brady had a personal fitness trainer, tactical coach, nutritionist, and sports therapist. He focused on every angle of elite fitness. If he had trained well but eaten terribly, he wouldn't have been physically, mentally, or emotionally fit to win seven Super Bowls.

Intricately and indelibly connected is every aspect of our being. So an individual, just as an athlete, who ignores the holistic approach to managing their money—relying only on limited factors and time—will be at a striking disadvantage to those who maximize their financial fitness by dedication to a comprehensive (holistic) financial regimen.

Pro basketball great Kobe Bryant is another athlete known for taking a holistic approach to his sports career. Some of his pre-game preparation, for example, involved meditation before shooting practice. His focused aim was on bettering himself to better his performances, doing every little thing possible to ensure he had an elite edge.

⁓ Meditation is like a gym in which you develop the powerful mental muscles of calm and insight, which you then use both in further meditation and in daily life to bring happiness and success.[49]
—**Ajahn Brahm**

Meditation is a holistic training tool used by several top world athletes to help them reach their "zone"—the flow state in which they perform at their optimal best, even in the most challenging situations. Here are just a few: Derek Jeter, five-time World Series champion; Misty May-Treanor and Kerri Walsh, beach volleyball Olympic gold medalists.

EMBODIMENT OF THE HOLISTIC APPROACH

Cambridge Dictionary defines holistic as "treating the whole . . . not just a part."[50] Our bodies with their multiple companionable parts and functions mirrors treating the whole. For example, our liver "breaks down, balances, and creates the nutrients"[51] yet it is holistically only one of the essential parts of the body. If we treat our livers well but neglect the rest of our body, not only are we limiting physical health but also mental and emotional health.

Our holistic being is a four-legged chair—physical, mental, emotional, and financial—and centered is the seat, our spiritual aspect. When one leg is not well-functioning and well-aligned with the other legs and seat, the chair is risky to hold any weight.

Elite athletes become elite by focusing on every aspect of their being—body, mind, and spirit. Why treat your finances—a primary aspect of your life that affects you physically, mentally, and emotionally—with less concern?

 ⁓ **Without peak financial health, you'll not be in peak holistic health.**

Taking a holistic approach to your financial life, you are also freeing your time and clearing your mind and spirit to gain the most enjoyment and peace in your remaining days and years. Sound like a dream? For those who dig in and take the holistic approach to their finances, it is a dream come true!

THE HOLISTIC APPROACH TO PEAK FINANCIAL FITNESS

The holistic approach to optimal financial fitness involves the collaborative efforts of your team of financial experts performing following tasks and more on your behalf toward achieving and maintaining your financial house's peak financial fitness. This list introduces you to the basics of the holistic approach.

Your team of experts, led by your trusted advisor, should have no conflicts of interest and should

> ‣ help you identify your most important goals based on your most closely held values and interests,

- ensure you have a specific, actionable, step-by-step plan to achieve your goals,

- tell you how much you should have in your cash reserves and where you should hold those savings to gain the most return,

- tell you how to keep those returns safe,

- manage your investments,

- look at every type of insurance that exists and tell you whether you need, and if you do, the specific right type(s) for you,

- hold you accountable, like a coach, and let you know if you're on or off track as time passes,

- be proactive in course correction—before you even know you're off track—and bring the solution to you rather than relying on you to bring the problem to their attention,

- give you comprehensive and complete instructions on how best to allocate your growth assets, including real estate, property, business, private equity, and any other asset intended to help you achieve your goals,

- ensure your tax situation is double checked and that you have every type of legal trust, strategy, or instrument you need right now while keeping an eye on your future, and

- much more.

As I shared earlier, holistic financial planning considers your finances in view of what's best for you overall as a unique individual—not simply as a consumer or money acquirer. This whole-person approach to your finances considers who you and your family are in every aspect of your life and desires and means devoting attention to every facet, making the best decisions to achieve the best results.

The difference between sports and finances is that in finances you're never competing with other people—only against your personal best! Athletes practicing a holistic lifestyle will focus on competing with themselves individually for personal betterment.

The lives of sports superstars who live holistically, like Kobe Bryant and Tom Brady, are elevated across the board and thereby have the winning advantage.

- The holistic approach to finance management includes every aspect: tax, insurance, investing, money management, and more.

- The holistic approach views each element of finance as vital parts of the whole financial body—just as the parts of the physical body are comprised of the whole human body, mind, emotions, and spirit.

- The holistic approach considers how each financial part is best set up and shaped to work optimally for your specific circumstances, lifestyle goals, unforeseen obstacles, end of life, and your legacy.

- The holistic process can give you ongoing oversight so you can wisely tweak any aspect as needed to guarantee your peak financial fitness.

THE FINANCIAL ADVISOR-COACH

Consider a professional baseball team looking to hire a head coach. They want to find the best. However, the franchise has no hiring process in place. The executive team doesn't know the best strategies to find and hire the best coach. Using this ego-driven mix of ignorance and bravado, they simply hope for the best as they fumble to find the best manager. Unless they get lucky, their chances of landing the best are slim to none. They end up hiring a coach who isn't well-fitted with the team's chemistry and needs. After a litany of poor results on the field, they fire the new hire and implement the same lacking process in search of another coach. And the insanity continues.

When we continue to make the same financial mistakes, not doing due diligence to understand, create, and improve our financial processes and hire the right people, how can we expect successful results?

We can't.

Does it make sense to apply time and energy to a less-than-ideal way of accomplishing something? Of course not. How much more an essential leg of our lives—our personal financial management?

Imagine consuming milk thistle to help your liver more quickly remove your alcoholic beverage from your system. Does taking milk thistle give license to throwing back ten shots of whiskey every day? Obviously not. Likewise, how do we stop ourselves from acting financially without thinking or without taking a balanced and benefiting approach to our financial health?

Stop doing what's not working and start doing what's proven to work.

As I shared in the introduction, many people hire various financial technicians, but that approach is not the same as building a comprehensive financial plan. For instance, talking to independent technicians (like a tax specialist and an investment manager), building a portfolio that's somewhat diversified, and buying insurance to protect your assets is not a holistic or otherwise high-standard approach. Holistic financial planning means considering every aspect of yourself, your family, your lifestyle, your goals, and your legacy—the powerful whole.

Let's say your goal is to ensure you have plenty of time to spend with your family and enjoy life—taking nice, twice yearly vacations and pursuing your golf, dog-breeding, and charitable giving passions. Does it make sense to continue working a job that requires you to put in twelve-hour days, six or seven days a week? No. This isn't to say that you can't couple working hard and enjoying life, but there are trade-offs of values and goals to consider. If your focus is to live an enjoyable and balanced life now rather than waiting until age sixty-seven, then working a job that consumes most of your time is not the way to go. Holistic financial management is.

The first and fundamental step to achieve the life you most desire is taking time to know, list, and understand your values and pinpoint which are most important to you, and to your spouse, and your family.

> *These are the keys that will unlock the door to personal excellence.*
> **— attributed to Confucius**

I often see assets not properly allocated, owners not benefitting from tax offsets, inefficiencies of improper insurance coverages and tax reporting, and many other issues. If you hope to make money, gain assets, and get your financial house in top shape, take the holistic route rather than betting on the silo method.

Elite athletes will keep the entire picture in mind by not allowing minor issues to distract them from achieving their primary goal. If a Grand Slam hopeful, like Sloane Stephens (2023), is to take home the prize, then entering a less prestigious tournament the week prior is likely not the best plan. Instead, she'll likely engage in optimal light training to stay energized and sharp and to avoid injury. In a 2022 interview, Stephens said, "I always take the time for self-care rituals . . . and consistently check in on my mental health through therapy. I'm vocal about what I need and what I'm feeling so people know and we can make a plan"[52]—little things that produce big outcomes.

Are you vocal in asking financial questions that can lead to big outcomes? Here are some examples:

> Have you asked your advisor, "How will changes in tax laws affect the decision I'm considering? Is this aspect of my finances coordinated with everything else we're doing?"

> Have you received specific financial advice and asked your advisor, "Is the advice right for me?"

> Have you wondered, *Is my advisor thinking of my next forty years or just today?*

> Have you wondered, *Is there a conflict of interest in the advice I'm receiving?*

What does one type of conflict of interest look like? For example, an advisor whose commission drives their advice.

What you need is an *advocate* with no conflicts of interest. A trusted advisor who genuinely cares about your financial goals and helping you work toward elite financial fitness to reach your goals and stay on top.

The sports comparison is the coach of an Olympic hopeful. The coach cares about the little things relating to the athlete's daily life and goals and creates a specific plan for the athlete to follow—the daily path to Olympic gold.

⌁ *The tragedy of life doesn't lie in not reaching your goal. The tragedy lies in having no goal to reach.*[53] — **Dr. Benjamin Mays**

If you desire to achieve peak financial fitness to achieve your goals, ask yourself these pivotal questions:

- What are my values, goals, and biggest dreams?

- Am I committed to taking a holistic approach with my finances?

- What does a holistic approach look like for my values, goals, and dreams?

- Where do I start?

There's a diversity of opinions about where to begin. I have an unorthodox suggestion: work on your physical fitness, whatever physical activities you enjoy. Why? Because, like the four-legged chair, your physical aspect affects the other aspects. Physical activity increases your health, longevity, energy, happiness, mental clarity, and focus, all of which contribute to your ability to stay on track to achieve peak financial fitness. Examples:

- If your work is demanding, staying physically fit is more likely to maximize your earning potential.

- Maybe you're not currently working, and you're looking for employment. The many benefits of physical fitness are vital to how well you will compete with other job applicants, for example, preparing stellar cover letters and nailing job interviews.

- Let's say you're retired or financially independent. Congrats! Your physical fitness isn't any less important. After all, what good does it do to work hard for decades, only to find that you're too unwell physically, mentally, or emotionally to enjoy the fruits of your labor or independence?

Regardless of your circumstance, there's every reason to devote time and structure to your physical fitness and to every aspect of your fitness, including financial. An important aspect of life is enjoying the money you've made! Few people will say that money alone is why they work hard and make sacrifices. For most people, money is a means to their desired lifestyle.

Do you really want to save money for five decades to not be able to enjoy the benefits? Do you want to be too tired or sick to experience the fruits of your labor?

No.

> **Money isn't the prize of a life well lived; it's a tool that helps you live life well.**

Exercise: Living to Age 100 and Beyond

1. Visualize yourself at age 100, still doing everything you enjoy. You're very active in your hobbies and community, you're still exercising your body, mind, and spirit, and maintaining peak financial fitness. You're traveling, living a great life with good health, surrounded by family and friends, and you have an amazing legacy to leave, including financial.

2. List all the things you need to do now and every day to come to ensure you're fit to live your dreams beyond age 100.

3. Examples, do you need to eat less, drink less, consume more water and vegetables, stretch and exercise more, sleep better, invest more in your relationships? Do you have a comprehensive financial plan that will ensure the fitness of your financial house beyond age 100 ?

➤ _____

➤ _____

➤ _____

➤ _____

➤ _____

➤ _____

4. Write what your optimal financial fitness and legacy look like to you:

_____

_____

_____

_____

_____

_____

You certainly don't want your money to run out along the way. This is called "longevity risk." As each year passes, technology and medicine improve and our average life expectancy increases. Some scientists suggest that our maximal lifespan may stretch to age 150![54] Planning, working hard, and maintaining fitness are required to ensure an optimal living for all of your years to come.

Even when you're fit in every way, financial decisions can be difficult to make, often involving complicated trade-offs between current and future spending, deferred gratification, future projections, and intersection with personal needs and desires. Making such important decisions, you're wise to enlist the counsel of a trusted advisor.

SPIRITUAL FITNESS

Essential to supporting and increasing your holistic health is your spiritual fitness—a leg of the chair. So, I encourage you to choose and use a spiritual practice, which doesn't have to mean a religious practice, though if that is your preference, great. By spiritual practice, I mean connecting yourself regularly (like diet and physical fitness) to thoughts that anchor you deeply in quietness, calmness, peace, and regeneration, better able to refocus with renewed energy and determination on the people and things in life that matter most to you.

Spiritual beliefs and practices, such as meditation, mantras, prayers, and journaling can help you quiet your mind, rejuvenate your spirit, and put the day-to-day struggles of your life into perspective.

Equally important, spiritual practices enable you to better see and focus on the countless positives of your life and the world and carry you into the richest place: **gratitude.**

Gratitude and maintaining such a powerful seat centered in harmony with the four legs of holistic health is powerful toward achieving any goal, like optimal financial fitness. Regular time spent in spiritual practice will help you maintain clarity and calm in financial planning, processing, entering your financial flow, and living an enriched life. Little things creating big outcomes.

Spiritual practices will help you realize that your *whole health*—body, mind, emotions, finances, and spirit—are central to everything you set out to do. Without a fit spiritual seat, the four legs of your being have no anchor, which risks harming and preventing your ability to achieve the life you most desire.

If you're unaccustomed to a quiet time of spiritual practice, I encourage you to begin with just twelve minutes a day in stillness. Little things that create big outcomes. My spiritual practice of choice, meditation, has a profound effect on me worth emphasizing. Since I started meditating, I'm calmer, more measured, more at peace, more grateful, more purposed, and more mindful.

Practicing meditation helps me make better decisions and take more decisive actions toward achieving my goals. Practicing meditation, I'm more knowledgeable about my values and purpose and more deeply appreciative of what matters most to me. And I'm more keenly cognizant of my blessings— my family, friends, purposed work that helps others, and good health. Being fit in every regard positions me to do the things I want to do—like writing this book and taking part in Ironman challenges.

MEDITATION AND YOUR FINANCES

Meditation is an ancient, proven practice that crosses religious and non-religious sects and individuality—meaning that meditation tools can include whatever context brings your unique mind into quietness and cleansing, your body into stillness, your emotions into balance, and a heightened awareness of all the great and small gifts in your life. Practicing meditation, in whatever context you choose, can open your eyes to the smallest wonders in life that create the powerful big picture of living. For example, a flower petal, the leaf, the stem that in unity with other petals, leaves, and stems creates the flower, which creates the garden, which in the broadest perspective creates the vast earth and all living things, embodying endless possibilities of health, wealth, peace, and joy.

Ray Dalio established and managed the largest hedge fund in the world. He credited meditation as playing a big part in his success. In his book *Principles: Life and Work*, Dalio shared how meditating for twenty minutes, twice a day, helped to reduce his stress, clear his mind, and consequently make better business decisions. Little things creating big outcomes. His advice?

> Meditate. I practice Transcendental Meditation and believe that it has enhanced my open-mindedness, higher-level perspective, equanimity, and creativity. It helps slow things down so that I can act calmly even in the face of chaos, just like a ninja in a street fight. I'm not saying that you have to meditate in order to develop this perspective; I'm just passing along that it has helped me and many other people and I recommend that you seriously consider exploring it.[55]

Spiritual practice promotes balance. Again, think of the seat securely balanced on the four legs of the chair. When you consider that the universe and all its elements are collaborative—in communication and working together and maintaining balance, you better appreciate the critical importance of maintaining your whole health balance of body, mind, emotions, spirit, and finances. Having a financial advisor, or you pulling together your team of connected, *collaborating* financial experts to work with you for your best interest, will help better balance your time, focus, and peace so you can do the things that matter most to you.

STAYING CALM

A principle of meditation is the calm factor. Disproportional emotions—like overacting and becoming overwhelmed—as opposed to remaining calm are both the result of our practices. Lack of maintaining calm is a sign that something within is out of balance and needs attention to realign. Rather than reacting disproportionally to setbacks and obstacles and allowing the sense of overwhelm, you can learn how to move into calmness and, with practice, maintain calmness through life's ups and downs.

Know that regardless of how fit you are of body, mind, emotions, spirit, and finances, you will have peaks and dips. So, regarding your financial house, you and your collaborative financial team must be calm, focused, and smart with your money. This doesn't mean your money will not encounter challenges but rather that no matter the circumstance, these principles holds true:

> ➤ calm enables focus

> ➤ focus enables smart thinking

> ➤ smart thinking will always serve you and your money best

When you have an elite plan and team, you're more likely to keep calm, make wise decisions, and stay on top—your financial house standing strong against whatever threats will come, and more so if you also have a head coach (financial advisor). Taking the silo approach to financial planning and management lacks the benefits of being surrounded and supported by a knowledgeable team.

An elite athlete will have learned from a coach and practiced how to remain calm in the center of surrounding stress, ensuring the athlete will be able to stay in the game and perform well. The same holds true regarding the practice of calm in readiness for the financial stressors that will come. I think of the phenomenon of calm within the vortex of a tornado and how that calm is not a halt of action but keeps pace with the velocity of the storm, as an athlete keeps pace with the velocity of aggressive opponents. Calm: a little thing that creates big outcomes.

PLANNING FOR THE FUTURE: TACTICAL VS. STRATEGIC

Those who take a silo approach to financial planning and management are more exposed to the damage of financial storms because they lack the expertise of information and strategies (all the little things) that can keep them (1) from heading into avoidable storms and (2) within the calmer eye of unavoidable financial storms.

Most people make *tactical* decisions rather than *strategic*. A tactical decision may be correct from a short-term or singular perspective but may be strategically suspect for the long term. Examples:

1. You've taken the silo approach and have successfully managed to set aside money for retirement, only to find (years later) that you need to use significant portions of that savings for unexpected circumstances due to later-life changes: a vehicle that better fits for your senior needs or a down payment for a home better-suited for your changing senior circumstances. The result of all your prior financial efforts is a retirement less satisfying than you had worked hard for and hoped for.

2. You saved for your children's college education using the 529 investment plan,* but your kids ended up not going to college or they got scholarships or attended in-state (lower tuition). What do you do with that 529 investment, since the earnings from withdrawals are likely subject to taxes and penalties?

   *A tax-advantaged savings plan designed to encourage saving for future education costs. 529 plans, legally known as "qualified tuition plans . . ."[56]

3. You deferred money to a retirement plan and the funds swelled to such a large amount that you ended up incurring estate tax or were forced to take withdrawals with high taxes.

   Many people fund a retirement account with the idea that they'll be in a lower tax bracket when they retire. But I've met many people who are in high tax brackets upon retiring. So, tactically speaking, it's good to set money aside for the future, but strategically you're better off putting your money into something that will help lower your tax bracket or may not be subject to future taxes.

Similarly is a pitcher who had a great season but convinced the manager to leave him in for extra innings. The pitcher's aim is to set personal records and win personal awards. Unfortunately, by the end of the season, the pitcher's arm was toast and his tactical mistake (pitching too much) ended up causing the team to fall short in the playoffs and cost them the World Series.

By following a tactical approach, you may win the battle by solving specific issues and gaining instant gratification, but the tradeoff is losing the war because you didn't step back to see the bigger picture. Another example:

4. You've maximized your retirement contributions for twenty-five years in a plan that allowed you to save as much as $40,000 per year. Your funds grew at seven percent over those twenty-five years and you have $2,529,961. That's great, except for the potential embedded cost at retirement time. When you withdraw from the account, you're taxed. The IRS considers the withdrawals taxable income, taxed at your monetary bracket. At tax time, in a $2.5M tax bracket, your financial position is a ticking tax bomb.

   The chart below shows your net after paying $1,486,352 in taxes. You'll have paid the IRS over $1M from your retirement !

   Interestingly, if you're young, looking at twenty-five years of work ahead of you, and pay the taxes now and invest the after-tax amount for twenty-five years, it can grow to be the same $1,486,352.

   Let's say you're a farmer. Would you rather pay tax on seed with a tax-free harvest or pay no tax on seed with a taxable harvest (depending on future taxes)? If tax rates were to remain the same, there would be no tax advantage either way because the net amount at distribution time would be the same.

Ask yourself: Do I think tax rates will go up or down in the future? At that future time, will I be in a higher or lower tax bracket?

You may be better off diversifying into more tax-efficient investments.

Other options include different tax-favored means that allow you to grow your money tax efficiently and have tax-free distributions. Do you know the options?

All the little things will either create big negative outcomes or big positive outcome—the reason to take a coordinated, holistic approach for financial planning and management.

Taking a comprehensive and coordinated team approach will optimize your chances of reaching your financial objectives. This doesn't mean the plan will magically enable you to achieve every goal you set, but a coordinated team approach can provide you with a more effective framework for meeting realistic goals.

Using the example of retirement planning combined with other goals, such as buying a house, a comprehensive approach might center on setting funds aside separately for each goal. This strategy reduces the risk of being blindsided in the future by a different financial need, hurting your chances of achieving another goal.

> **If you spend a dollar on one goal, that's a dollar you can't spend on another. Understanding this is key to making realistic, smart, achievable plans.**

The overarching point behind holistic financial planning is that every aspect of your financial life affects every other aspect. Wouldn't it be best—safer, calmer, more enjoyable and peaceful—if all the little things were managed expertly toward creating big positive outcomes?

> *You must gain control over your money or the lack of it will forever control you.*[57]— **Dave Ramsey**

Examining the world of elite athletes, it's easy to see how a single-minded approach can be counterproductive. Consider the football wide receiver who focuses on his speed but doesn't practice catching the ball. He will probably sit on the bench until he realizes that running fast on the track may be enough, but not on the football field.

Or the baseball pitcher who puts all his effort into throwing as fast as he can but pays no attention to throwing with control. The pitcher will probably have the same negative results and may hit the opposing batter with stray balls. Being unable to keep the ball in the strike zone means that no matter how fast the pitcher throws, there are likely few outs to record.

Moving out of sports and into your neighborhood—like the following photo—let's look at the holistic approach to financial planning and management as building your custom home. Would you begin by erecting the walls? Of course not. Would the first step be to pour the foundation? No. How about first gathering the building materials? No.

The first step is to hire a professional architect to draw up the specific plan of details that aligns with your circumstances, vision, and goals. Assuming you're not a trained architect, does it make sense for you to create the blueprints? Logically, you'd delegate that task to an expert.

If you expect to have a well-built home, will you serve as the general contractor or hire a trained and well-seasoned contractor with a proven track record in home-building? What's logical and smart is for the contractor to coordinate all the needed experts and collaboratively move in a flow state to build your home. All the little things create big outcomes.

When construction begins, will you disappear to Tahiti for the duration? No, your essential part in building your home is to talk with, listen to, and learn from the home-building experts and make critical decisions in face-to-face collaboration that will ensure your team understands "all the little things" you desire while trusting them with "all the little things" of their trade that together create a big positive outcome.

> *There is no such thing as a self-made man. You will reach your goals only with the help of others.*[58] — **George Shinn**

Building a solid financial foundation is essential before making speculative investments (high-risk) in tech, biotech stocks, crypto, NFTs, commodities, or precious metals. Not to say there's no place for such investments in a balanced portfolio.

If you're prepared to take the risk, you may want speculative, but do you want to bet your retirement fund strictly on high-risk assets? Probably not. A trusted advisor will know the risks and advise you on the best investment plan for your circumstances and goals.

Just as an elite athlete will build a foundation of focused fitness and hone the basic skills of their sport, establishing your financial basics with a focus on financial fitness is advisable before developing advanced techniques, riskier expenditures, and speculative investments. The holistic approach in athletics and finance means considering all the little things toward big success.

The parable of the three little pigs applies to everyone and to every aspect of our whole-health fitness—body, mind, emotions, spirit, and finances. As I shared earlier, many people think their financial house is solid, but what they actually have is a financial house of wood or straw. What's worse is not knowing that there are financial bricks that will exceedingly improve your life and what those bricks are. An expert financial advisor will know the bricks and how to best to lay and secure those to help ensure the protection and growth of your financial house.

Essentially, the key question is this: What kind of financial house do you want when the big, bad wolf appears at your door? Or a natural disaster or other economic downfall?

What's clear is that having a well-planned financial house built on the solid foundation of holistic principles is the best way to withstand the unexpected.

 What you get by achieving your goals is not as important as what you become by achieving your goals.[59] —Zig Ziglar

Although you need a variety of skilled tradespeople to build a custom home, those workers need a leader—an experienced general contractor—to ensure that all the little (and big) things needed are in place and at the right time and the goals are accomplished correctly and with excellence. The best team will provide oversight that is free from conflicts of interest with your best interests in mind.

In sports, the coach is like a general contractor. There are many examples of talented teams that never win a championship because they haven't achieved a collaborative flow with a strategic plan. Creating synergy is the coach's job, and the best coaches know how to combine players' talents to serve the team and goals optimally.

Likewise, a proven and trusted financial advisor will strategically orchestrate and oversee your financial plan and ensure that you and your financial team stay on track and perform at peak fitness for optimal success in achieving your goals.

Though you may not yet be able to hire that advisor, you can gather and apply expert advice from books, research, seminars, and classes. Either way, expert help will allow you to conceptualize your life goals and devise your custom financial plan that's sound. A source is *CFP: Let's Make a Plan!* at www. letsmakeaplan.org/how-to-choose-a-planner.

SUMMARY

> All the little things matter.

> Taking a comprehensive, holistic approach to your finances is the best way to reach peak financial fitness.

> Drawing inspiration from the holistic practices of elite athletes and financial advisors can help you build a solid plan, get into a financial flow, and remain calm in the face of challenges.

CHAPTER THREE
The Mental Game: Flow, Resistance, and Failures

May what I do flow from me like a river,
no forcing and no holding back, the way it is with children.
— Rainer Maria Rilke

Danny Way set out to achieve a goal no one had yet accomplished: a jump over the Great Wall of China. On a skateboard.

Yep, Danny Way had dreamed big. He saw possible what seemed impossible. His 2005 record-breaking success started in his mind—a vision and then a determined mindset. He took enormous leaps (literally) over the wall and broke two world records (and his ankle), breaking one of set records three times![60] In an interview afterward, Way said, "The mind is very powerful. . . . I had the mind over matter attitude."[61]

To achieve his extreme endeavor, Way had needed to go deep into his flow state. "The skateboard is so much my home," he shared in another interview, "it flips a switch in my brain and autopilot takes over . . . and all these things release"—like thoughts of the injury he'd sustained the day before his record-defeating feat.

The wall was just one of many obstacles Way had needed to prepare himself to overcome physically and mentally with unshakable confidence, just as he had been practicing consistently for years, conditioning his mind, body, and spirit to unite in a state of flow. Just building the ramp jutting out from both sides of the Great Wall had taken Way and his team of experts seven months to construct. All the while, Way continued to maintain his elite fitness of body and mind. He believed in his team and his team believed in him, having no doubts that he would accomplish what he'd set out to achieve in Beijing.

And he did! Despite his fractured ankle!

Way was the first skateboarder to successfully jump the Great Wall of China, and at its widest point, and surpassed his previous record.

Just like Way and other elite athletes find the mindset and other means to achieve what appears to be impossible, so can you. Anyone one of us can achieve more than we think possible.

In Steven Kottler's book *The Rise of Superman: Decoding the Science of Ultimate Human Performance*, he made an astute observation:

> To really achieve anything, you have to be able to tolerate and enjoy risk. It has to become a challenge to look forward to. In all fields, to make exceptional discoveries you need risk—you're just never going to have a breakthrough without it.[62]

Once you experience financial flow, you'll want to maintain that, especially against life's unexpected financial downfalls. Gaining and maintaining financial flow can give you more time for new opportunities, adventures, ventures you're most interested in, peace of mind and financial security.

When the mind and body are in flow, we act from a well-refined and conditioned place within us, all five of our human aspects united and flowing like a river. Your earnings flow smoothly—organized, protected, and working well for you and your family and legacy. Your money can grow through sound investments, like a rising, branching, sprouting, and reseeding tree that withstands the elements and time. And the right insurance (part of achieving financial flow) can protect what you need and want in times of unexpected personal challenges, natural disasters, and market fluctuations.

The flow state is a term coined by Mihaly Csikszentmihalyi, pioneering cofounder of the positive psychology field. His definition of a flow state is when "a person is completely focused on a single task or activity. . . . directing all of their attention toward the task, . . . [without] many thoughts about themselves or their performance." In his book *Flow: The Psychology of Optimal Experience*, he explained:

> *A person who has achieved control over psychic energy and has invested it in consciously chosen goals cannot help but grow into a more complex being. By stretching skills, by reaching toward higher challenges, such a person becomes an increasingly extraordinary individual.[63]*

Csikszentmihalyi defined *psychic energy* as "attention" and said,

> *The optimal state of inner experience is one in which there is order in consciousness. This happens when psychic energy—or attention—is invested in realistic goals, and when skills match the opportunities for action. The pursuit of a goal brings order in awareness because a person must concentrate attention on the task at hand and momentarily forget everything else.[64]*

As Csikszentmihalyi put it: "The purpose of the flow is to keep on flowing, not looking for a peak or utopia but staying in the flow. It is not a moving up but a continuous flowing; you move up to keep the flow going."[65]

The emotional feelings of living in financial flow are part of rewards; peace of mind, freedom of spirit and time, and security are powerful feelings. This doesn't mean you'll somehow be exempt from the harsh realities of life and your unique emotional makeup. Way, for example, felt nervous but confident and determined before his physical leap across the Great Wall of China. When the time arrive to take that leap, his mind, body, and emotions merged as one—the flow state—feeling calm and completely clear-headed.

You are your own unique individual. A fact for everyone is that achieving the flow in any regard—athletically, relationally, financially—will take ongoing effort and intent. If flow were an equation, it'd look like this:

~ **Competence + Challenge + Goal-Setting + Commitment + Practiced Action = Flow**

The flow state is optimal engagement of every aspect of your being toward a big goal and bigger goals and financial flow is your money working for you as a financial fit house.

Flow does not come easy, but it's optimal for gaining and remaining on top of your goals, as we've seen in athletic examples.

MENTALITY AND YOUR INNER VOICE

We each experience times when the voice in our head is our opponent, telling us lies like, "You're not good enough. Your dream is crazy. You can't achieve that goal." And too often that inner voice acts as a high court judge, the gavel slamming down hard against our desires, and we mistakenly believe that inner voice is the final decision maker. That inner judge takes every opportunity to assume the bench of authority in us. We not only harshly judge ourselves, but also others.

Our inner judge, like all things in life, has two opposite poles of reign. On one end, your inner judge will throw you into your inner prison and throw away the key. On the other pole, your judge will set you free of heart, mind, and spirit to become all you desire to be. The truth is, you—each of us—get to decide which judge you'll elect and from which pole the judge will preside. I think we all want to live on the pole that frees us to be all we can be and extends grace and help to others.

The first step toward gaining and maintaining our best mindset is to catch that negative judge in the act and send it to a different bench—to sit out of the game, like a coach will bench the athlete who's not performing well or behaving well. Stay alert, mindful, to keep the best inner voice in play.

I like to call my inner condemning judge Darth Maul, from Star Wars.

～ Imagery is a powerful tool toward being our best and maintaining flow.

Darth Maul is the red and black Sith Lord and his weapon is a double lightsaber. When I hear him launch into negative talk in my head, I picture my freeing voice as Luke Skywalker, with Jedi powers that overtake and conquer the inner enemy of darkness and doom.

The imagery allows me to reconnect with who I'm always at work to be: my best in every aspect—financially, physically, and mentally, emotionally, spiritually, and relationally. Not only relationally well with others, but with myself.

Important in every regard is not allowing your Darth Maul judge to win but being mindful to keep Luke Skywalker ruling. I'm sure Danny Way, at least at the beginning of his extreme sport journey, had to work to silence his Darth Maul and instate Skywalker to conquer the jumps that ultimately led him to leap over the Great Wall of China.

Great Wall of China. Peakpx. Creative Commons Zero - CC0 Used with permission. (illustrated from)

Whether your financial wall is high, low, or midrange, practicing to maintain your jedi mindset and flow will help you conquer anything you choose and any challenge that confronts you.

MINDSET CHECK

~ **The right mindset is the entryway into flow.**

When a sportsperson's performance looks effortless, though it's extremely technical, they're likely in their flow state. If someone is making their money work for them—their financial house in shape and generating passive income—they're likely in financial flow. Behind both scenarios is a positive and growth-oriented mindset.

Legendary golfer Jack Nicklaus said, "I feel that hitting specific shots . . . is 50 percent mental picture [visualization], 40 percent setup [goals], and 10 percent swing [taking action].[66]

Ask yourself these important mindset questions:

> ‣ When I have a setback, a fall or failure, what is my typical mindset?

> ‣ Do I bounce back stronger or stay down for the count?

> ‣ What was my mindset during the COVID-19 pandemic? Was I self-starting or stuck?

> ‣ Is my faith as big as my vision or does my faith and attitude waver?

> ‣ Am I consistently becoming stronger or weaker in any aspect—emotionally, physically, spiritually, and financially?

> ‣ Are my goals dialed in or derailed?

> ‣ Am I powering through or have I lost my drive?

> ‣ Do I typically believe I have more or less opportunities?

Consistently keeping your mindset in positive check and practice, you'll naturally grow and experience the fruit of your flow.

MINDSET STRENGTH TRAINING

Try the following 12-minute mindset-strengthening exercise. You may gain (1) a greater ease of ability to more quickly and often move into your flow state, (2) an improved focus and concentration, (3) a heightened positivity and calm, and (4) a greater motivation to follow through with your goals.

Such results are seen in the performance of elite athletes, in artists (music, painting, photography, and other arts), exercise, business, and other activities of accomplishment, including financial fitness.

I challenge you to test this mindset exercise for ten consecutive days:

Exercise: 12-Minute Flow

With a timer, dedicate 12 minutes to this exercise.

1. Pick up a *non-electronic* object you like.

2. Sit with it and set the timer.

3. While taking slow, deep breaths, examine the object with sight and touch.

4. What textures does it have? _____

_____

5. Does the object feel cool or warm? _____

_____

6. How does the object make you feel physically? _____

_____

7. How does it make you feel emotionally? _____

_____

8. Write more about your focus experience. _____

_____

_____

_____

_____

_____ Repeat daily.

Because I'm confident in the results, I also challenge you to make this practice part of your daily regimen.

A strengthened mindset of positivity, focus, and growth is a winning mindset.

There's a saying in sports: Champions are made, not born. While there are many talented competitors, winners are those who understand that mindset matters most. A champion's mindset allows us to get the most from our talent and training (the grind), even in the face of highly stressful, challenging circumstances.

The brain is a powerful thing.

A 2021 report by *CNN Sports* cites a joint research project of the British Ministry of Defense and Dr. Samuele Marcora, developer of a psychobiological model for endurance sport. Two groups of soldiers were given the same physical task and one group was also given a mental puzzle. In a subsequent endurance test, the group that was challenged with both the task and the puzzle lasted three times longer.[67]

I was at the University of Houston for the 2021 PAC 12 Women's Swimming & Diving Championships to watch my daughter compete as a freestyle sprinter for UCLA. As I entered the Campus Rec & Wellness Center, the chlorine-infused air smelled strangely comforting. I had grown up swimming indoors in Central Illinois. The chlorine air wafted into my brain and drew out some good and less-than good memories of swim practices. Competitive swimmers must practice every day or their skills will decline.

At the college level, swimmers practice twice a day, putting twice as much time into the pool, conditioning their bodies to move as trained—in the flow state, their minds not having to think through each movement. This elite state of mind and motion is how you want your money to work for you: effortlessly.

When my daughter finished the 50-yard free swim, there was a post-swim interview with the winning Stanford swimmer, Anya Goeders, who was asked, "What was going through your mind at the start of the race?" Anya answered, "Nothing." Her ability to silence her mind and allow her well-trained body to move naturally made her performance look effortless, like a dolphin gliding, poised in excellence.

An untrained swimmer will move like a fish out of water—thrashing around and having to stay focused on every movement to ensure they stay afloat.

That's why the phrase "stay afloat" is so often used in context with people's financial condition. Hypervigilant and often floundering as they live paycheck to paycheck, barely keeping their heads above water. Most spend their entire adult lives trying to stay afloat and hoping they can keep dog-paddling, somehow, through their work years and retirement.

Elite athletes dedicate themselves to everything that's needed to condition their minds and bodies to move as one, in peak performance, without the interference of thoughts.

In your financial pool or ocean (it doesn't matter the size), are you a thrashing fish, caught up in the net of debt or caught by the hook of poor advice? Or are you a dolphin, effortlessly enjoying your life as you flow gracefully toward your next adventure?

A 2023 article reported that sports neuroscientist Dr. Izzy Justice had studied over 10,000 brain scans, comparing the neuro-activity of professional golfers to amateur golfers. His aim was to understand what state of mind resulted in a successful golf putt and what state of mind put a golfer on a poor-putt trajectory.

> The results of his research are very clear that when we play closer to our potential, our brain activity is much quieter. Our brain wave frequency in effect slows down to a level allowing the communication between brain and body to function at an optimum level. When our brain is 'busy' with the intensity and frequency of our thoughts, we literally clog up the pathways from brain to body and dramatically reduce the likelihood of success.[68]

How can we gain and maintain a winning state of mind? The many factors include these three:

> ‣ The ability to remain mentally calm amid chaotic environments that can evoke uncertainty and fear—think pandemic and economic downfalls, for example.

> ‣ The practiced mindset that a setback is simply a temporary pause on the road to success.

> ‣ Practicing flow in a mindset of commitment and contentment through tough times—pushing through with gratitude.

On the J.P. Morgan returns chart below, consider the orange "average investor" column. The average return is only 3.6% compared to ten categories with higher returns. What does this chart tell us? Money invested in equities, like stocks, did almost three times better—10 percent over the same period.

How can that be?

With the right, practiced mental flow, an investor can avoid becoming emotional and making sabotaging choices against their financial hopes and goals. All the more benefitting, of course, is having the advice of professional investment manager or financial advisor.

Regarding the column "Average Investor," note that a person's age is a factor that can affect financial decision-making.

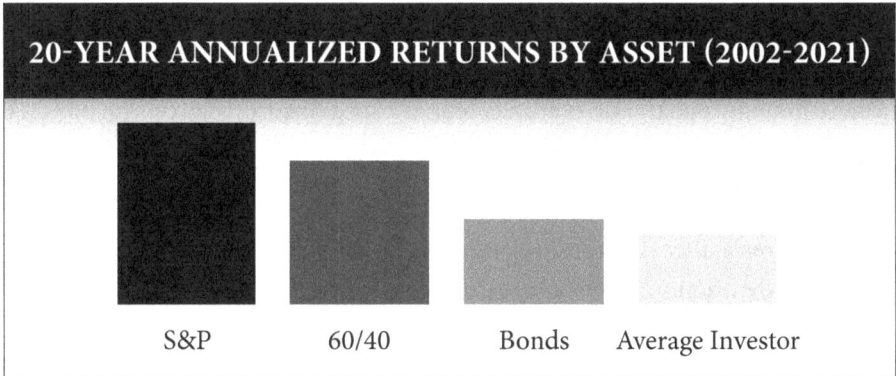

20-YEAR ANNUALIZED RETURNS BY ASSET (2002-2021)

S&P	60/40	Bonds	Average Investor

Younger adults are more likely to make financial errors because of inexperience and are typically more impatient, wanting to cash in earlier than the average older adults. But younger adults are more likely to be fluid in changing circumstances whereas older adults are typically less cognitively flexible. While less-flexible thinking can cause financial mistakes, older adults are typically more experienced in financial decision-making and more patient, waiting for bigger payoffs. Older adults are also less likely to react emotionally to changing circumstances.[69]

ATTAINING THE FLOW STATE

Countless studies and the achievements of elite athletes and other high achievers have proven that calming practices like meditation—that quiet the mind, body, and spirit—help to ease stress, stabilize thoughts, and increase focus. Each of these outcomes is essential to attaining the flow state, which is essential to excellence and superiority in achieving goals.

> *The goal of meditation is not to get rid of thoughts or emotions.*
> *The goal is to become more aware of your thoughts and emotions*
> *and learn how to move through them without getting stuck.*[70]
> **— attributed to Dr. Phillippe Goldin**

In athletics, meditation is often closely linked with visualization: performing an athletic feat with the same calmness you experience when meditating. But how does visualization with a calm mind work in finances?

When you're calm, collected, composed, accepting of whatever life throws at you, and focused on the vision of your desired lifestyle and legacy, you're more likely to make solid financial decisions that work for you.

Along with our efforts to maintain flow, we must be mindful of our *resistance* to feelings and circumstances that can disrupt or block our flow, keeping us from achieving a goal. For example, fear is a foremost resistance.

In his book *Do The Work*, Stephen Pressfield's focus is on overcoming our resistance to success. He described resistance as a dragon we can slay and identified resistance by these examples: "fear, self-doubt, procrastination, addiction, distraction."[71] He addressed fear of success as "our greatest fear"[72] and explained his theory:

> When we are succeeding—that is, when we have begun to overcome our self-doubt and self-sabotage, when we are advancing in our craft and evolving to a higher level—that's when panic strikes.[73]

Pressfield dismissed that idea that our feelings of inadequacy is our "deepest fear" and wrote, "Our deepest fear is that we are powerful beyond measure."[74]

Take a moment to consider that truth and the bright light of implication: our possibilities are limitless.

Also consider Pressfield's "Rule of thumb: The more important a call or action is to our soul's evolution, the more Resistance we will feel toward pursuing it."[75]

So how can we slay the dragons of our resistance?

Proven weapons include:

> ▸ meditation—quietness of body, mind, and spirit

- movement—physical activities and exercise, and

- medium—creative expression like dance, poetry, painting, and other art forms.

"What will keep us from stopping? Plain old stubbornness," says Pressfield.[76]

1. Start with a plan, outlining what you hope to achieve (macro and micro goals).

2. Think big and limitless.

3. Believe in yourself and your goals.

4. Do the work—research, education, application, seeking wise advice.

5. Stay motivated, committed, and determined to holistic fitness: body, mind, emotions, spirit, and finances and overcoming obstacles and resistance.

You have grand destinations!

RESISTANCE FOR PEAK FINANCIAL FITNESS

Let's say that you keep an eye on your spending and all other areas of your finances. Still, there are temptations lurking that your trusted financial advisor will probably warn you to resist. Here are a few examples.

1. Trying to time the market to sell high and buy low. Missing the timing can severely impair your returns. A recent article (2023) in the Wall Street Journal warns: "*Market timing is almost always a loser.*"77 Far safer is focusing on the long term. Yet when the market becomes volatile, many investors get nervous and sell out, even though their objective is long-term growth. Over the long run, this fear response can harm your financial results in the same way an athlete who consistently skips practice and goes on binges will have difficulty performing at their best.

2. Lacking proper insurance, organization, and safe storage. Purchasing insurance is a crucial part of a comprehensive financial plan—risk mitigation. While an event that triggers an insurance policy may never occur, it's important to have that protection in place and important to have a trusted insurance expert to help you determine what insurances

you need and the detailed factors that align with your particular needs. Proper insurance coverage will help to ensure your financial house is protected against harmful events. Considering such events, it's also vital to have all of your financial documents well-organized and physically protected, which I'll discuss further in a later chapter.

∼ **To be financially fit, you have to put in the work.**

3. Taking the financial advice of non-experts. You may have a trusted advisor but we all encounter financial salespeople or friends and family who can't resist giving us financial advice. While the advice may be right, what's essential is that you have the financial plan that's best for you, guided by a trusted financial expert. Resist the temptation to assume that what others are doing or the non-professional advice they're giving is best for you and your unique circumstances.

∼ **Resisting potential financial pitfalls is essential to protecting and growing your wealth.**

STAY FOCUSED

Pro golfer Sergio Garcia won the Masters in 2017. The next year, during the first round to defend his title, he made an 8-over-par 13 on hole 15, hitting the water ten times. In the end, he carded a historical octuple-bogey.[78] Was failure the end of the story? No. Sergio resisted the past, rallied by staying focused, and birdied the next hole!

While athletes and investors need to learn from past mistakes and successes, focusing on the present moment, resisting past failures, is key to putting those lessons into action.

The stock market has winning days and losing days. Real estate gains and loses value. In private equity opportunities, some investments win and others lose. Life is a series of ups and down, and like a pro surfer, we must focus practice on the flow, riding the waves. Past mistakes and fluctuating markets don't faze the sophisticated investor who's maintaining focus and flow with a dedicated team of experts. The opposite of flow is rigidity, which every pro golfer or surfer knows can evolve into resentments that rob them of the present moment of opportunity.

In the investment world and in my team's work for clients, we analyze a completed project to determine what we did well and areas we can improve with focus. We pass the past and focus with optimism, calm, clarity, and confidence on what we've learned and what we can change to be better at surfing the waves and aiming down the fairway of the market.

SUMMARY

- Gaining and maintaining the flow state enables you to achieve your best, fully invested in the present task.

- The more your mind is focused in a flow state, the more your finances will flow.

- When your financial house is in elite fitness, your money does the work for you.

- Passing the past and overcoming resistance will help you maintain your flow in each aspect of your being and life—mentally, physically, emotionally, spiritually, financially, and relationally.

Get out there, and get flowing by following the principles outlined in the next chapters!

CHAPTER FOUR
Set Goals by What's Most Important to You

Success is simply a matter of luck. Ask any failure.
— Earl Wilson

My Interview with Allison Schmitt

Multiple Olympic gold medalist Allison Schmitt seemed to have been born with an acute understanding of the nuances of goals. While big and little goals are fun and inspiring to envision, achieving those is not a matter of luck.

Allison loved swimming as a kid, and at age nine joined a swim team. But her heart and greater focus were on soccer. She gave her all to soccer and when she didn't make the team, though disappointed, she dived into her other love with equal dedication—the pool of competitive swimming. "I had that drive inside of me," Allison shared, but "there were definitely some ebbs and flows."

She also described herself as having "that dedication . . . to keep working" toward her goals, which meant being organized, disciplined with her time, nutrition, and mental balance. "It's definitely about understanding what *I* could do," she emphasized "I" and said she went into practice every day with the mindset of doing the best she could do with the knowledge she had. The best she could in nutrition, recovery, and training.

Allison emphasized the value of having support. "Having that team that's going for one goal really helped me to stay focused . . . on what I needed to do every day to get better. I'm going in, I'm showing up, and I'm doing the best I can do. But I'm also relying on my support system. I'm relying on my trainers, masseuse, coach . . . And I'm also relying on my family, my friends for support." In reflection, she added, "I really understand the support system and relying on others, but [also] doing the best you can do with what you're good at. I was going to do the best I could do in my own training to get to that goal. When I'm standing on that podium, I know that it's not just me . . . , that gold medal is not just mine, it's the whole team's. They had a part in helping me get there."

Looking back on her achievements, Allison said, "Success made all the work and all the obstacles . . . worth it."

Before nationals, one of her micro goals was to shave seconds off her time. Though she was "pulling 1.04s" (64 seconds), her coach gave her the belief that she could do better, "hit another level and . . . keep training to hit that level."

Micro goals. Allison proved by her successes that those little things matter.

Regarding finances, many people have audacious goals, like the second home—on the beach. But the mindset must be in the day-to-day financial goals, the incremental goals that will take us all the way to our big dreams. Allison concurred, "It's a little kid saying, 'I want to go to the Olympics.' Well, at ten years old," she laughed, "you're not going to the Olympics! There's a lot of stuff in between. If I sat here today, and I had $100 dollars in my bank account, and said, 'I want a million dollars,' . . . it's those little steps in between and setting those little goals."

Celebrating the little goals helped Allison push through to gold. "Being humans, we like to celebrate. It keeps that motivation going; it keeps that hunger alive within ourselves. . . . Celebrating those little goals makes you hungry for more."

Reaching her big goals was more about competing against herself than competing against others. At her best, Allison was also the most consistent. "Consistency is huge, no matter if you have those downfalls or the highs."

I asked her what was going on in her head as she moved forward to reach higher levels of personal excellence in her sport. "Belief," she said without hesitation. "Understanding that you can't put a limit on yourself. Life happens [but] you're the driver. You are in control of how hard you push and what you push in. There really are no limits in what you can achieve."

Incremental goals, the small goals of focus, carried Schmitt forward from the time she was a kid in the slow lane at team practices. She made a friend at the pool who was more advanced and training in the fast lane. Allison's motivation to work harder was to join her friend in the fast lane.

She wasn't thinking about medals; she was driven by what she most valued—

training alongside her friend. Her small goal toward that bigger goal was simply to touch the feet of the person in front of her. "That was my game," she said. "I'd swim up to the person ahead of me and touch their feet"—a heads up to let the swimmer know you're about to come alongside them and move in front of them.

"Eventually, I was moving up in lanes. I used that as a game. That was my every day stepping stone. Every day I'd want to try [to] touch someone's foot to get higher into the lane or to get into the next lane. I'm huge into games like that. I like to keep things interesting; I like to keep things fun. And I also know how hard you have to work in order to achieve your goals, so I have combined them . . . What can I do in this little picture to achieve a bigger goal?"

Allison made it to the fast lane.

She got to train alongside her friend, and the rest is record-breaking history.

Allison rose to become an elite athlete, passing others and winning medals because she loved competing against herself, setting micro goals and achieving those. Having fun competing against herself, challenging herself in the small goals, eventually led her to the Olympic podium, wearing the gold medal. In fact, Schmitt was a four-time Olympian, and at this writing she still holds the 200-meter freestyle American Olympic record she hit in 2009. Allison won twenty-five medals in major international competitions—thirteen gold, nine silver, and three bronze—facts I rattled off during our chat.

At the heart of Allison's success is her passion: "I love swimming!" she said. "I love the sun . . . the overall health I get from swimming, both physically and mentally, plays a big role on my day."

In planning our finances, we must do so from what means the most to us. Our genuine passions create our dream visions and both fuels us forward to achieve those.

Perhaps your passion is oil painting and your vision is to open an art gallery to showcase the work of other artists alongside your own. Maybe, like me, you're passionate about athleticism and desire the financial means and time to travel in pursuit of that passion. And perhaps life's hits have dimmed your flame, like it eventually did in Allison.

She had gone public about her ongoing battle against depression. I asked her how swimming has helped her emotionally and mentally. She said, "Everything is ebbs and flows," and recommended, "pick a few things you can focus on."

"I call that 'gamification,'" I interjected.

Schmitt replied with a hearty laugh, "I guess I never really put a term to it!"

At the 2012 Olympics, Allison set a record and won the gold, but she went home feeling low, emotionally "different," she said. Although she was very grateful for the life she was leading and for her supportive family, education, and success, she felt depressed, but didn't know that her symptoms were signs of depression. She didn't know much about mental health or how to grasp why she was feeling so low, and she kept the darkness to herself, considering all the wonderful things in her life. She felt that if she said anything, she'd come across as complaining.

Yet the prevailing darkness inside her continued to steal her joy. Allison shared with me the thoughts that had gone through her mind as silent pleas. "Can someone please hear me? Can someone please understand me? You can have these medals; I just want my happiness back."

Two years later, January 2015, she reached an emotional breaking point. She was embarrassed and felt bad for the people who were worse off than her. In May that year, her cousin, also an athlete, age seventeen, committed suicide. "It helps [my struggle] to spread her story. Allowing people to know [suicide's] not the only answer. . . . Allowing people to know that it is okay to not be okay, but it's not okay to isolate." She continued with compassion and plea, "I know that the hardest step is to ask for help, but it's the best tool in your toolbox … to ask for that help."

Allison shared that her experience battling depression and urging others to ask for "inspired me to go back to school and get my master's in social work, so I can work with athletes" suffering from mental health challenges.

At this writing, that's exactly what Allison is doing—she's in school and working in mental health internships, hitting micro goals toward the bigger goal to help change the stigmas around mental health. "We have to continue to work at that," she said, having made great strides with her own mental health work and being open about her emotional struggles and needs. "Being venerable isn't a weakness but it can help you succeed, not only in your performance but in every area of your life."

I asked Allison if swimming helps her with depression. "Swimming has saved my life," she answered. "Having that structure has saved my life. In my darkest times, knowing that I still had a responsibility to show up for my teammates . . . on those hard days. There was so much juggle going on outside my [personal] life that swimming was the constant . . . and a safe place."

What an example of how living in our passions and setting goals in those can help us endure through our challenges.

Schmitt also understands that everyone is different, has different needs, and we must make our decisions based on what's best for us as individuals rather than leaning toward others' expectations. This truth returns us to the importance of viewing our finances from the perspective of what is uniquely best for us.

What are your particular needs and what do you most want for our life now and for your future? It's not about trends; it's about what's tremendous for you personally.

One of the best reasons to stay in constancy, a flow of setting and achieving micro goals (the little things) in every area of your life, is to achieve and maintaining peak whole health—mental, emotional, physical, spiritual, and financial. That constancy in achieving micro goals naturally leads us to achieve our major goals, even in the worst of times.

> Apply dedicated goal-setting, micro and major

> Have fun achieving the micro goals

> Celebrate each achievement

> Be present in every moment (focused on micro goals and micro wonders around you)

> Stay in the healthy rhythm you've trained yourself to enter—the focus and automation that propels you forward and sustains you even in the toughest times.

That flow state, which I'll discuss further in the next chapters, is an essential practice to achieving peak results. Psychologist Csikszentmihalyi put it this way:

The best moments in our lives are not the passive, receptive, relaxing times . . . The best moments usually occur if a person's body or mind is stretched to its limits in a voluntary effort to accomplish something difficult and worthwhile."[79]

As Schmitt showed, following her passion and staying enveloped in that passion was an essential part of managing her struggles with depression, and she was motivated to excel at her sport because her sport was her passion.

When you have a heartfelt, passionate reason behind a goal, you have many advantages. Here are just four:

1. The power of the passion behind your goal creates a higher likelihood of achieving that goal.

2. The power of the passion behind your goal will help you persevere through tough times.

3. The power of the passion behind your goal leads to what is most fulfilling along the journey.

4. The power of the passion behind your goal will play a key role in boosting your mental and emotional health and healing.

∼ Taking small, constant steps achieves goals, not simply saying, "I want to win the gold."

Let's equate that principle to retirement goals. When someone tells me their financial goal is to retire at a certain date, I ask them to spell out that goal. Typically, I hear that the goal is financial freedom with a specific amount in the bank and a calendar date. I then ask what their thoughts and feelings would be when they reached their goal.

∼ Connecting your goals with your heart, your passions, is the stronger motivator than the goal itself.

I asked Allison for one word that describes her success, and she gave me two. "A mixture between consistency and support [through] all of life is ebbs and flows," she added. "Find that consistent factor that we're in control of to help us reach that end goal and not get too high [emotionally] if we reach a goal, but not too low if we don't reach that goal by certain deadline."

CONSISTENCY AND SUPPORT

To achieve major goals in life, whether in athleticism, finances, or gaining that beach house, you gotta have consistency and support. For example, when we get lost in our heads about the ups and downs of our investments, we can lose sight of our goals and lose our motivation. Maintaining consistency and support are key to moving through whatever is happening around us and inside us and reaching our micro and major goals.

ATHLETES AND GENERAL GOAL SETTING

When an athlete sets a goal, they think of the

> - reason behind the goal,

> - how much the goal means to them,

> - the practicalities of the goal, and

> - what they need to do in micro steps to achieve the goal.

Once you decide to take a holistic approach to your finances, the next step must be asking yourself what personal values of depth are behind your goals that will help you achieve your goals. Answering that question before diving into the pool of financial details is essential to avoid ending up in the wrong lane and down the road faced with making major changes because your plans didn't match your values, your passions, and your innate purpose.

To determine the values driving your finances, you must ask yourself what type of life you honestly want to live now (your current micro goals) and in your future (your dream goal). When targeting a future goal, ask yourself pertinent questions that will get to the heart of the matter. An example are questions about retirement:

> - How much of my current income am I willing to set aside to fund my future retirement lifestyle?

> - What value does money serve in my life? Do I value money to fund my lifestyle? To support my family? As a marker of success?

> - How much do I value maintaining financial security over taking financial risks?

For answers, let's explore personal growth as the highest value. Every day offers us the option to grow as a human being, which is all about uncovering who you are at the deepest level—your most authentic self, formed of unique gifts, traits, and desires. Regardless of how much wealth you've accumulated or what businesses you've sold or how many gold medals or other championships you've won, most important is knowing who you are now and what type of person you aspire to become in mindset, emotions, and spirituality, which are fundamental to your physical and financial aspirations.

⮑ **Your goals are not solely about the big dream, but the opportunities to better yourself along the journey.**

As exampled by Allison Schmitt, focus on being better today—in every aspect of your life and being—than you were yesterday. With this constant mindset, you'll likely find that you're becoming more fulfilled in the moment, day by day, as Allison found to be true as she focused on touching the feet of swimmers ahead of her. Her focus was on the micro goal of the moment that naturally led her to her heart's desire: training alongside her friend in the fast lane.

Life, goals, finances, sport, personal growth, are about the journey, not the destination.

WRITING TO REALIZE YOUR GOALS

⮑ **A goal not written is more often not realized.**

Whether with pen and paper or your electronic device, writing your major goals and breaking those down into written micro-goals is the first *physical action* toward making your dreams a reality. Writing also promotes motivation, organization, and accountability. When you write something down, it feels more real because you've performed a physical act toward the goal, comparable to an athlete gaining muscle memory: "The ability to repeat a specific muscular movement with improved efficiency and accuracy that is required through practice and repetition."[80]

A good example is legendary tennis champion Chris Evert. From an early age, her father drilled into her the principle of dedicating herself to constant practice if she wanted to be the best tennis player. Her devotion to practice cemented her physical ability to keep the ball in play—a flow state achieved by muscle memory—and wear down her opponents. The muscle memory she'd built over the years propelled her to victory after victory and reaching the peak of her potential and the sport of tennis. That level of muscle memory ensured her excellent performance.

While it's unnecessary to rewrite your financial goals repeatedly, the physical acts of writing, revisiting, and tweaking your goals are physical actions that motivate your mind and spirit to achieve each, and with more stamina and consistency, and organization.

Writing your financial goals is also similar to athletic training in terms of commitment level. Evert didn't simply think about tennis; she and her coach committed to the first physical steps to achieve the sport—a plan, likely written.

Writing your financial goals increases your level of commitment, motivation, accountability, and organization to take the physical steps to achieve those.

> *Most people don't plan to fail but fail to plan.* —Unknown

After writing your big goal and micro goals, the next physical step is to write a realistic completion date for each. As you're pursuing a written goal, you may find that you need to change the date. This isn't license for perpetually changing a date to give yourself free passes to keep putting off the goal; that premise returns us to the importance of knowing your passions and what you most want in life based on what you most value. Otherwise, what will motivate you to have goals, much less deadlines? As life happens, part of maintaining a healthy balance is being *pliable* and treating goal dates realistically.

> **We're motivated by passion and moved into strategic action by writing.**

Be specific in listing your goals and micro goals. At this stage of planning, you're not concerned with *how* you're going to reach the goals, but *what* your goals are and seeing them in writing.

First, list from your heart everything that matters to you in terms of goals. Don't limit yourself; dream big! Then ask yourself, *What's important to me about success?*

1. Write five of your heart-rooted life goals.

   1. _____

   2. _____

   3. _____

   4. _____

   5. _____

2. Thoughtfully determine the priority of each, rewrite the goals in that order, and write beside each a realistic achievement date.

   1. _____ _____

   1. _____ _____

   1. _____ _____

   1. _____ _____

   1. _____ _____

   In your personal development journal, take this exercise a step further by breaking each goal into micro goals and assigning achievement dates to each. Then hit the grind! You can do whatever you set your heart and mind to!

Someone once told me that if comfort is your goal, success is not in your future. Whether you plan for the future, it's coming. Do you want to be a person who sits back and lets life happen, wait to see what fate will hand you, or are you a person who plans your path, optimizing your ability to live the life you most desire?

I believe this timeless adage:

~ *Hard choices, easy life; easy choices, hard life.* (**Unknown**)

◦ The greater danger for most of us lies not in setting our aim too high and falling short; but in setting our aim too low, and achieving our mark.[81] —Michelangelo

Lots of people in business follow what's called the 40 percent rule. Here's the idea: when your mind tells you that you're at your absolute limit, completely done, you're actually only 40 percent of the way.

I've experienced that phenomenon in training and competing in Ironman competitions—competing to exceed my perceived limitations. When my mind told me to give up, and I kept pushing, I discovered that I was nowhere near my limit. Had I not pushed myself beyond my perceived ability, I wouldn't have known my true capability. That's a truth worthy of repeating:

◦ Pushing yourself beyond your perceived ability reveals your true capability.

So, dreaming big, what financial goals should you set for yourself? Your answer will be unique from other people's if you're tapping into your heart and uncovering your values and passions. The list of possibilities is endless, but here are some common goals—financial or otherwise—in no particular order:

> ➤ financial independence

> ➤ sending kids and grandkids to college

> ➤ taking a special trip every year

> ➤ flying first class or private

> ➤ funding a scholarship for your alma mater

> ➤ establishing or helping to fund a charity

> ➤ commissioning a building, such as a hospital, community center, or place of worship

> ➤ giving away most of your wealth, keeping just enough to achieve your other goals

> ➤ living on the road or a cruise ship or in a Tuscany farmhouse for a year

> ➤ living healthy to age 100 or beyond

- learning an instrument, learning it well, playing in front of an audience

- learning a language and traveling to that culture to use it

- memorizing poetry

- writing a book

You can calculate how much you should save from each paycheck to reach a particular goal, but you're probably not going to arrive at a sum that's 100 percent accurate. Why? Determining savings for big goals is a trained skill, best delegated to a financial expert. The financial technician can run all the numbers and explain all the variables involved, such as inflation and market volatility, depending on your goal and what you can afford. By all means though, go ahead and do the calculations to have a general idea of the sum, and know that a trusted expert will be able to refine the calculation with more accuracy.

BEING PREPARED: THE PIANO GUY

A few years ago, my wife and I experienced an amazing cruise on a small ship designed for 200 passengers. Every cabin was a large suite with a large patio and an amazing view. We cruised the Baltics and ported in St. Petersburg, Russia; Tallinn, Estonia; Stockholm, Sweden; Helsinki, Finland; and other historic locales. The trip was one of our favorites for many reasons, and one of my coolest memories was the piano guy.

All 200 of us were facing an unexpected two-hour delay to disembark. Many of us settled into the beautiful open atrium between the ship's four levels to wait. The delay to disembark was a recipe for passenger impatience and stress. But a passenger intervened. Impromptu.

He hopped onto the atrium's grand piano bench and began to play fan favorites that were awesome sing-alongs. Tunes by Elton John, Steve Miller, Billy Joel, U2, David Bowie, and others. The atrium's acoustics lifted and swirled the sounds and carried them into all the upper and lower decks.

As soon as his fingers hit the keys, the atmosphere sounded like everyone aboard had joined in singing. We continued the singalong for nearly two hours.

One individual, the piano guy, had 'double-handedly' changed the mood trajectory of 200 people for the better, not because he had *planned* to do so, but because he was already *prepared* to do so, not knowing that such preparation would be so valuable. He created a valuable experience for his fellow passengers, using his talent and an unforeseen opportunity. "Carpe diem"—he seized the moment to make a difference because he could.

What's the point?

We can write all our goals and the micro steps to achieve them, but if we don't walk those out with focused time and dedication to planning (piano lessons), enlisting support (piano teacher), and practicing, we won't be as prepared emotionally, mentally, and otherwise when life throws us into unexpected scenarios—good and bad—as it often does.

Think investments and Ponzi schemes, like Bernie Matdoff.

Think unexpected highs and lows in the market, like The Lost Decade, or an inheritance.

Think athletes and unexpected victories, like the New York Giants (underdog) defeating the New England Patriots in Super Bowl XLII.

Think unseen and unexpected, like Allison Schmitt against depression and the piano guy against the mood of 200 people.

> When the Giants defeated the Patriots, when Schmitt defeated emotional darkness, when the piano guy defeated the ship's potentially sinking atmosphere, they each already had in place the preparedness that made victories possible.

An essential part of training and enlisting help in pursuing goals is being *preconditioned* to rally through the unexpected and come out shining, whether in a championship game or on a cruise ship.

⁓ *precondition: to put in a proper or desired condition or frame of mind especially in preparation*[82] —**Merriam-Webster**

1. The piano guy had an original goal—to learn to play piano and memorize all those songs.

2. His support team had likely been his parents, the piano teacher they enlisted, and peer piano students.

3. His process had to have included exploring his likes and dislikes, leading

him to plan what songs he truly wanted to learn to play and memorize. He didn't wake up at age eight with the magical memorization of his repertoire, nor could he have known that life would present him with the opportunity to jump in and save the day.

4. He dedicated himself to preconditioning by learning the fundamentals, practicing those, and rising in skill.

5. He apparently learned how to move his mind and body into a flow state, and had likely put his skills to the test by consistently entering various performances—otherwise, he wouldn't have been so prepared when his fingers touched that grand piano on the cruise ship.

Years later, in that moment of serendipity, the piano guy was prepared to step in and use his skills to make a difference, in other people and himself. That became part of his legacy, just as the Giants' grit and gain and Allison Schmitt's grit and gain became part of their legacies.

THE POWER OF FINANCIAL GOAL SETTING AND SEIZING

My chest sinks when someone tells me they've hit all their goals and have nothing else to shoot for.

Goals hit should lead to creating more goals. Why? Because we're not done in life until our last breath.

A professor stood in front of his class and pulled from his briefcase a pint-size glass and a can of beer. Much to his students' surprise, he then pulled from his case some golf balls and dropped them into the glass, filling it past the brim; a couple of balls rolled out.

He asked the class, "Is the glass full?"

They responded, "Yes," of course. Then he pulled from his case a pouch of sand and poured the particles into the glass, in and around the golf balls, until the sand overflowed.

"Is the glass full? he asked again.

Hesitant, yet certain of what they were seeing and now knew to be true—the glass hadn't actually been full before—they answered, "Yes, it's full."

The professor popped the beer can's tab and began pouring the beer into the glass, which the sand eagerly consumed, filling the nooks and crannies around the golf balls and granules to the tip of the glass. He held it up and said, "First, don't put golf balls and sand into your beer glass!" The class laughed and the professor said, "Now it's full."

> The golf balls represent your important goals.

> The sand and beer represent everything that's taking up space in your busy days.

> The point? If you first fill your time with all the busy stuff, there's no space remaining for the important goals that dwell in your heart and occasionally tap at your mind, reminding you they're still there, waiting for you to give them proper space and time.

~ **Your important goals are your prime directives and everything else should be fitted around those.**

Thinking you're done in life—no longer needing to set and achieve goals—shows that you've lost sight of your inner spark and need effective rescue steps:

1. Grab a notebook and pen.

2. Carry those to your favorite spot at home or outdoors—that quiet place that makes you feel good, at peace, safe, and offers you a renewed spirit.

3. Take a series of deep, slow breaths.

4. Then, consider what interests or possible new interests you haven't yet experienced.

5. Start writing your list. Here are some example goals and walking them out:

   • Hop online and visit your local community center's list of classes and sign up for one or two that interests you. This avenue, and all the following examples, also leads to meeting new people, which naturally creates further new opportunities.

   • Try a new hobby. When you find the one you like, look for a local group that meets regularly to enjoy the hobby together.

   • Volunteer differently—at a different location and take on a task that's new for you. I'm assuming you've already been volunteering somewhere. If so, it's time to mix things up a bit.

- Call a music store and sign up to learn an instrument. You never know when you'll find yourself in a two-hour delay on a cruise ship with 200 passengers and a grand piano calling your name.

In Kenny Chesney's song "Get Along," he wrote:

Paint a wall, learn to dance
Call your mom, buy a boat
Drink a beer, sing a song[83]

Never doubt the power of goals: financial, tangible, abstract—anything.

There are far more people who are new to goal-setting than the handful who have reached all their goals and need the rescue steps. Either way, those steps should be a consistent writing exercise in our lives.

I still have my diary from 1993, which contains a list of my life goals. I wrote the list while sitting on the balcony of a family friend's condo near Magic Sands Beach Park on Hawaii's beautiful Kona coast. It was my first time in Hawaii and I felt inspired by the sound of the waves and the beauty of the sunset. I was age twenty-three, and ripped through identifying and writing down my major goals. The list included how much money I wanted to make at that time and over time, my desire to travel internationally, at least annually, the type of relationships I wanted, how many kids, and so on.

At that age, I didn't know who I truly was beneath all the layers. I just knew that travel, seeing the world, and having other experiences were important to me, which made the financial aspect of my goals critically important. Remember that everything we do and desire has a financial component that's either direct or indirect—it's a leg of our life's chair.

So, did writing my goals help me achieve them? Absolutely.

Writing my goals actually helped me exceed them! I'm living the life I could have only dreamed of: a wife, three kids, over fifty trips to foreign locations, a wealth management business, and more. My dreams became realities because of that moment I took to write down my dreams. That action ignited me to pursue my goals, as though my ink pen was a matchstick, the paper a torch, the ocean a sea of limitless possibilities, and the sunset my witness.

Returning to the previous goals exercise in this chapter, go to your inspiring, peaceful spot. Breathe deeply. Dig deep through your interests and passions. Strike your pen to paper, writing and igniting your goals.

Whatever walk of life you're on, formulating your goals in writing will help to motivate and organize you to take the next steps to achieve those goals. There are many examples of athletes who named seemingly impossible goals, and over time, with action, focus, training, and experts, realized their dreams.

Set all of your goals with excellence in mind. This doesn't have to mean multi-millionaire with bucket loads of disposable income. Set goals that are truly meaningful to you. Examples: taking a family vacation every year may require you to save an extra $30 per week. Funding college for your children may mean juggling a side hustle with your primary job.

Regardless of your particular desires, the likelihood that you'll achieve those becomes greater when you identify your goals, write them down, and take the next step.

Believing in yourself and your goals is equally important. Professional triathletes Kelsey Withrow and Jocelyn McCauley had the following to say about the journey of achieving:

> Kelsey Withrow: If you work really hard and believe in yourself, despite the odds, dreams can come true. It just takes a lot of work.[84]

> Jocelyn McCauley: It was almost two years in the making to be able to win an IRONMAN. It took a lot of learning as a new professional triathlete as well as many other investments, particularly a lot of time. It also took a lot of belief in myself and in the process.[85]

Every year I set new goals with the belief that I'll achieve those—ranging from financial, athletic, health, and relational, to spiritual.

In 2013, I set a goal to do my first Ironman. As a busy dad, business owner, husband, and coach, I knew it would be hard to find the time, but I went for it. I set the big goal and incremental goals and worked hard to achieve them. Completing that first Ironman wasn't the end; it was a personal invitation to set a new goal: compete in the Ironman Kona World Championship. Although that goal was so far out of my conceived ability, I took one step at a time, beginning with writing the goal.

Ask any elite athlete or other high achiever who wants the most out of life and they'll say goals aren't set to hit and then quit. Goals are gateways to the next achievement.

Goals are dynamic. We can view them as living, brimming with life, and ever-growing because at the root of goals is action. Goals need attention and nurturing. You hit the goals on your list, your confidence grows, and you set new goals. Those that you don't hit, you amend and keep moving.

> ∼ **It's better to set a mountaintop goal and get halfway there than aim halfway and only make it to the quarter mark.**

Likewise, approach your finances with that goal-setting, goal-writing, and goal-achieving mindset and actions.

Financial goals in your twenties may look different in your thirties, and aspirations germinating in middle-age may take a different shape in your sixties and eighties. So, writing and amending goals will be an ongoing practice.

Typically, most people gain their wealth in their fifties and sixties because of changes in their saving habits, business building or selling, inheritance, and general financial trajectories. Some of the most interesting people I've met are those who continue to set new

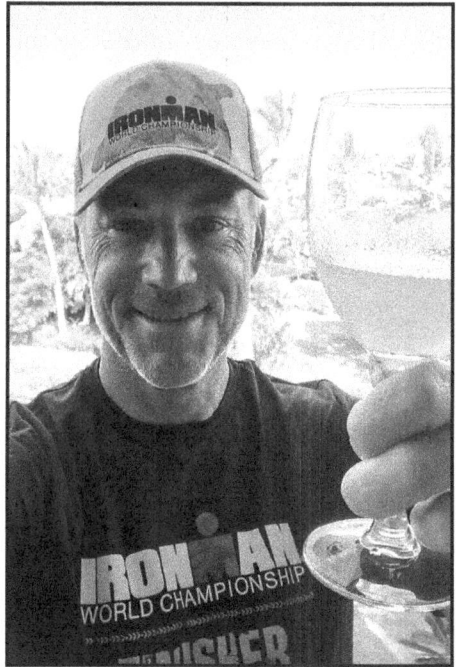

Darren Wright at Kona Ironman 2017

goals throughout their years. For example is Nancy Kinney, an aged woman who deeply inspires me. At this writing, she's ninety-four and her aim is to swim three times per week in the Phoenix Swim Club Master's program. Whether it's bone cold or blazing hot in Arizona, Nancy never misses her swim schedule. Not even the COVID-19 pandemic held her back.

When wealthy people think their money is protected (immune from financial risk) simply because they're sitting on $10M or $100M, their minds have become "hubris"—overly self-confident about their financial position. They think their financial house is surely at least a 7 on the financial fitness scale, and some believe they've "made it" to the peak, sitting at a 10.

In reality, their financial fitness is probably a 5 or 6. As we've seen, it's possible that wealth can disappear overnight. Rewind to Bernard Madoff's Ponzi scheme: $64.8 billion defrauded from folks who'd taken a backseat view of their finances, enjoying the ride while allowing someone else to take full control of the steering, speed, and navigation of investors' financial plans. The investors had become comfortably complacent about their financial fitness.

Other examples include doctors, notorious for thinking their medical knowledge has somehow qualified them as investment experts. Why? High achievers can become hubris—doctors who have adopted a God complex that carries over into their financial management. The results can be disastrous. You can be a brilliant brain surgeon, biochemical engineer, award-winning actor, best-seller author, elite athlete, and so forth, with little clue how to best safeguard your money and make it work best for your short-term and long-term goals.

Professional athletes and artists (high-profile musicians, actors, and models, for example), are more often prone to bankruptcy, especially after retirement or a high streak. Some find it difficult to restrain their spending after their income dramatically drops. Many neglect to consider the unexpected: a sudden lay-off, a major accident, a serious illness, or their unethical or immoral choices that are suddenly exposed and instantaneously shuts down their careers.

A few years ago, I had a phone conversation with a sports personality to provide him with financial guidance. Let's call him Boxing Joe. He was earning hundreds of millions when competing for boxing titles (in addition to endorsements and other modes of income). He was earning a lot of money. But his net worth shrunk over time to $2M—an unbelievable low compared to his heyday earnings.

What happened to Boxing Joe's money? Mistakes, hangers-on, poor deals, taxes, and a host of other small and large actions that systematically sucked his income near dry.

The missing component? Joe hadn't taken the time and effort to ensure his financial house was in shape and strong, in peak fitness to withstand life's storms. Like many, Boxing Joe thought his high bank balance would carry him like a magic carpet through the rest of his life.

It's not that Joe paid zero attention to his finances. He was complacent. He didn't pay enough attention to his financial house, nor enlist a team of experts to guide him and help ensure his financial house would remain standing strong. Had Joe gathered a trusted financial team to help him steer, navigate, and watch his spending speed, he would have likely continued to enjoy the standard of life he once had and preferred.

Financial disaster, loss of income, is not exclusive to the wealthy but can happen to any individual across the earning spectrum. Every day, there's a new financial crises that appears in someone's life—a serious health diagnosis, death of the primary breadwinner, a layoff, physical or financial accident, a hurricane, a poor investment, a global pandemic.

> **Whether you have $5K or 10M, do not be complacent about your financial fitness!**

Ensure that your financial house is in peak fitness, no matter what you're earning or how much you've saved. The goal, regardless, is reaching and maintaining a 10/10 on the financial fitness scale:

> - Know yourself and your desires.

> - Set goals based on who you are and what you desire.

> - Write those goals.

> - Share all the above with a financial team of experts, or best a trusted and trained financial advisor managing the team.

> - Revisit your goals regularly and tweak as needed.

> - Hit goals consistently, step by step. It's not a race; it's realism.

> - Create new goals consistently.

For how long? Until you take your last breath.

By our nineties, we're well into the realm of what our financial legacies will look like for our children and for others we want to leave endowments, and we're well past the mode of teaching our children how to set and maintain financial goals for their optimal financial fitness.

Regarding teaching our children, imagine having spent eighty years of your adulthood carefully attending to your financial fitness and leaving a healthy legacy to your children, only for the funds to be quickly flushed because you had not taught and shown your children how to become and maintain peak financial fitness.

MARGIN OF SUCCESS: STAYING ON TOP

A proven principle in elite athleticism is this:

~ **Staying on top requires significant effort, even for those with tremendous natural ability.**

Sometimes, it's the small margins that keep us from achieving our dreams and on the flip side, the small margins can propel us forward to success—for example, one of your investments paid big time or a financial book you read made all the difference in achieving your goals.

From the standpoint of both competitive sports and finances, there's a narrow margin between success and failure. For instance, according to a 2023 report, there were only 3,619 professional-ranking tennis players in the world.[86] Of those, only the top 400 to 500 players can make a living at the game.[87]

Vasek Pospisil, 2014 Wimbledon men's doubles champion, said "The most common struggle for anyone ranked outside of the top 100 is financial, and the stress it causes." ESPN cited.[88]

In the game itself, victory can be determined by one or two points in a match that can last for hours, emphasizing that the smallest margins can separate winners from losers. Pros know the margins and the hard work necessary to stay on top. Michael Jordan would stay after practices and shoot free throws. He didn't just know the following universal law but also filled his margins (time, focus, micro goals) with this principle:

~ **If you don't work to be better, you become worse.**

Legendary NFL running back Walter Payton strengthened his iconic thunder thighs by consistently running up and down the Mississippi levees in off-seasons. The payoff was that he could bust through the wall of defensive players like breaking a chain of rag dolls in a game of Red Rover. But his primary competition was himself. He worked hard in training to surpass his perceived limits, knowing there was always another dimension he could reach, and ranked at the top of his game.

The distinction between a peak performer and everyone else is the performer's commitment and diligence to remaining in the grind, continually pushing and growing, even in the smallest margins—like Allison Schmitt shaving seconds from her 1.04-minute time.

That mindset on margins applies to gaining and managing wealth. If you're making money but you aren't continually in the grind protecting it down to the narrow margins alongside your best-in-class advisors, your hard-earned success is at risk.

James Clear, #1 New York Times bestselling author of *Atomic Habits*, wrote, "If you get one percent better each day for one year, you'll end up thirty-seven times better by the time you're done."[89]

SETTING TANGIBLE AND INTANGIBLE GOALS

He who is fixed to a star doesn't change his mind.[90]
— **Leonardo da Vinci**

Let's say you really want that beach home I mentioned as an example to Allison Schmitt during our interview. That's a tangible goal you can fix your eyes and mind on. Some of your micro goals along the way may need to change, which is part of the journey toward achieving big goals. You may find along the journey the need to set intangible goals to ensure you ultimately gain the key to your dream beach home.

An intangible goal is any mindset change you need to make to gain your goal. You may not believe that your dream is possible to achieve, and with that mindset, you're far less likely to take the tangible steps—financially and otherwise—to become the owner of the beach home.

As you're achieving your micro goals toward gaining the beach home, you'll face risks like inflation, taxes, and varying returns. Such risks should not prompt you to change your tangible goal but prompt you to change your financial goals when and where needed over time to attain the tangible goal.

Other tangible goals, like education and retirement funds, must also be continually monitored and updated to stay on course, because these goals will inevitably get off track. You can hand this delegable task to a trained technician, which is generally the best way to check your goals' feasibility.

∽ **The goals you fear most are often the ones you should aim for.**

Sometime earlier in my life, I told myself I'd never go skydiving. However, one of my intangible goals was to conquer my fears. So, I knew what I needed to do: skydive! That tangible goal wasn't something I had dreamed of doing; I went skydiving because I didn't want to! The thought terrified me. So, pushing myself to reach my intangible goal (overcoming fear), there I was one day, at 13,000 feet in the sky, standing at the open door of a moving plane, armed only with my parachute backpack, and I jumped out.

My wife (Pam) and I had flown to Dubai to skydive—downtown. We jumped from 13,000 feet over the Palm (in Dubai). The location is known as one of the most epic dives because the jump takes place above the tallest building in the world, Burj Khalifa, which stands at 2,717 feet, and then jumpers float above the huge man-made island.

I free fell for sixty seconds and then floated for five minutes to the ground.

As I was free falling, my heart thumped rapidly, the air pressure stretched my face, and as I hit terminal velocity, time seemed to slow to a crawl and I entered total calmness and focus. At that moment, I heard an inner voice say, *Darren, you're conquering your fears and pushing yourself beyond your perceived limitations!*

Upon landing, my emotions overcame me. I had pushed through my fear!

> What experiences are you telling yourself to avoid?

> What's holding you back from those experiences?

If you don't know the answers, I challenge you to dig deep within yourself to find out.

If you're saying anything like "I'm good. I've achieved my goals. I'm set," you're likely suffering from a limiting mindset. If so, I urge you to reach deep to uncover all that's meaningful to you now and for your future. Then set those goals in writing, push through fear or whatever you've discovered is the obstacle, and defeat it with this mindset:

∽ **I can. I will. I am doing it!**

Do it. Gather your support team and accomplish your goals.

Trainer Tim Grover (who helped Michael Jordan and Kobe Bryant) wrote

Relentless: From Good to Great to Unstoppable, about his training philosophy and methods. Grover included mantras he attributed to the most successful competitors, whom he called "cleaners." Among the mantras are these:

> You keep pushing yourself harder when everyone else has had enough.

> You don't recognize failure; you know there's more than one way to get what you want.

> You don't celebrate your achievements because you always want more.[91]

If you're shying away from committing to the grind of achieving elite financial fitness, ask yourself these questions:

1. What will you achieve by pushing through?

2. Who can you enlist to help you?

3. How can you further help yourself?

Now, believe in yourself and consider hiring a trusted advisor to review all your financial documents. Also assess with your advisor other aspects of your life that complement peak financial fitness and list those in your financial plan. You and your advisor need to know everything about your habits and hopes in order to design and build your unique and strong plan. For optimal financial fitness, you must be willing to share with your advisor

- ▸ what's important to you about money,

- ▸ why you want money, and

- ▸ what that money will help you achieve,

- ▸ listing your present and future goals, tangible and intangible.

These and other such questions and actions bring us full circle, back to your values. Some people pursue money for security, others for freedom to pursue their dreams, others for the sake of seeing how much they can accumulate, and other reasons.

∼ Our values drive our desires and actions.

Consider the emotional power of these example values:

> independence

> pride

> providing for family

> making a difference in the world

> personal fulfillment

> balance

> spiritual growth

> inner peace

> self-confidence

> self-worth

Such examples are called "level three values."

You have a much better chance of achieving your important goals when behind each goal is a big "Why?"

∼ From the place of deep spirituality (introspection), you'll find your mission or calling.

Everyone has level three values, but not everyone gives those values much thought. Those who are less aware or unaware of their level three values are likely settling for less in most aspects of their lives, including financially.

Consider your tangible goals and how each will benefit you. Study the example goal worksheet. Then, choose one of your tangible goals and complete the blank worksheet that follows this example:

EXAMPLE GOAL WORKSHEET

Description of Goal	Financial Freedom
Amount Needed to Finance Goal	$50,000 Monthly In Today's Dollars After Tax
Completion Date of Goal	May 11th 2030
Intangible benefits (how will it improve your quality of life from an emotional / psychological standpoint)	Peace of Mind, Accomplishment, Security
Tangible benefits (how will it improve your quality of life from a material standpoint)	Do what I want for me and others when and how I want it.

GOAL WORKSHEET

Description of Goal	
Amount Needed to Finance Goal	
Completion Date of Goal	
Intangible benefits (how will it improve your quality of life from an emotional / psychological standpoint)	
Tangible benefits (how will it improve your quality of life from a material standpoint)	

Dreaming big is important, but many people get stuck between their end goal and their ability to achieve the goal. I call this "the void." People living in the void are there because they haven't set incremental goals that are realistically achievable. The result is their loss of motivation and gaining disappointment and defeat. Some then falsely and resolutely think, *It just wasn't meant to be.* Such beliefs are not only limiting but excuses and untruths. What's "meant to be" is anything you set your heart and mind to the grind and achieve.

The void is why writing your goals, breaking those down into micro goals, assigning due dates, and celebrating each achievement are essential.

Achieving micro goals builds the bridge between desire and destination.

> Bridging the void is also part of living a *balanced* lifestyle.

> Achieving realistic micro goals and celebrating each also generate momentum and motivation that will ultimately lead you to reach your most ambitious goals.

An example is Elon Musk's hefty goal to transport human beings to Mars. Talk about big goals! But look at his history. He has steadily set and met goals that propelled him to achieve greater goals. And he didn't stop. Setting goals, pushing through the grind, and moving in a flow fed his sense of purpose, challenged him, and grew his knowledge and confidence. What an extraordinary life of elite experiences! Why not Mars? Why not shoot for your billion-dollar bank account? Why not aim for tennis pro and Olympic gold? Why not go for Ironman and skydiving? Why not aspire to visit every country in the world? Why not write a book or twenty-five books?

Perhaps there are goals deep within you. Taking a step back to pause and think about what's important to you can lead you to discover buried goals that are waiting to be released. Whatever inspires you, write it down and just go for it.

CHOICE AND WILL

Just as Allison Schmitt didn't look behind her but focused on the swimmers' feet in front of her, to signal that she was going to pass them, we must pass our pasts and fully focus on the present and future.

Maybe you shared a dream with someone who replied, "Well, good luck with that!" Or perhaps someone rolled their eyes and said, "You need to be more realistic."

In every cohort of family and friends, there's usually at least one card-carrying member of the cold-water committee. No matter what you want or why you want it, they'll be front and center to tell you all the reasons you can't or won't make it.

Prove them wrong. Never allow naysayers to hold you back. Pass them on your way to your dream!

I never had much confidence growing up. I spent a lot of time playing with army men and action figures and built elaborate cities from cardboard boxes, old toy parts, metal scraps—anything I could find in my basement. I had a monetary system and entire story lines going. I did these activities alone, which was my way of dealing with my inner voice saying, *I can't do this or that.*

Although I was picked last for dodgeball, sat the bench in baseball, wasn't great at conversation, had below-average grades, not a bunch of girlfriends, but awkward moment after awkward moment, I did have a mom and dad who believed in me. My mom was a tough woman who built a multi-million-dollar business, bought out her partner, ballooned the business even more, and sold it across multiple cities in Illinois for a big number—and at an early age. And she never had to work again. She taught me to dream big and goal plan. She's the reason, the influence, for my hardwired base to achieve most everything I've written down to this day.

◠ We are each solely responsible for our outcomes.

It's easy to take the route of blaming others for why we're not amounting to much. But as adults, we each make decisions that push us forward or hold us back. Here are five examples of legendary athletes and artists from among many who were told to quit, or that they didn't stand a chance, or something equally false, or experienced a stream of failures.

> › Babe Ruth, though not an orphan, was schooled at St. Mary's Industrial School for Orphans, Delinquent, Incorrigible and Wayward Boys because his behaviors were "delinquent, incorrigible, and wayward."[92] He was known for his strikeouts but worked hard, stayed in the grind, and

ultimately set baseball records, exceeded those, and became a legend.

> Muhammad Ali failed the "tale of the tape" test in every category and was told he didn't have a future in boxing. Through his relentless pursuit, he became known as one of the world's greatest boxers in history.[93]

> Dennis Rodman was among the most rejected; he even tried football before he pursued basketball. He became a pro, a record-setter, and was inducted into the Basketball Hall of Fame.[94]

> Lionel Messi was told he was too short to play soccer, and he was cut from his junior year team, yet he reached soccer stardom.[95]

> Kurt Warner, Football Hall of Fame 2017, was kicked out of the Packers' 1994 training camp, took a minimum-wage job at a grocery store, and worked his way back to the NFL.[96]

> World-famous artists who fought their way forward and reached the stratosphere include The Supremes, Janis Joplin, AC/DC, Madonna.[97], Morrissey, U2, Sheeran, Gaga, Beyonce, and . . . The Beatles.[98]

Pass the past and don't allow any unbelief from others, yourself, or your present circumstances to embed your heart and mind. Unbelief and limited beliefs are like a virus. It will slow you down, set you back, and can even halt you altogether. Take charge over your mind. The best antivirus to help ensure you reach your goals includes:

> taking care of yourself in every way,

> fixing your eyes on your dream,

> setting and achieving incremental goals,

> remembering who you are: able, and

> believing in yourself.

There's a simply stated but profound statement in the movie *The Shawshank Redemption*, delivered by the character Andy Dufresne (Tim Robbins) and also Ellis "Red" Redding (Morgan Freeman):

⤳ *Get busy living or get busy dying.*

Most everything in life boils down to personal choices and will. Between the vibrant life and possibilities brimming around you and your inner power, purpose, and gifts, you have everything you need to create the life you most desire, imbued in peace and happiness. What are you going to do with it all?

SUMMARY

As we've seen, there's enormous value in setting goals, basing them on what's most important to you, writing your values and goals, breaking goals down into micro goals, celebrating, believing in yourself and your dreams.

> ➤ It's up to you to determine your values and set your goals accordingly.

> ➤ Personal growth is an essential value; always work toward improving yourself and pass the past.

> ➤ Set and write lofty goals and micro goals to get you there.

> ➤ Orchestrate your financial planning to support each goal, every step of the way, and consult with your financial experts.

> ➤ Celebrate each achievement and that as the beginning of conquering your next goals.

> ➤ Be prepared, thinking like the piano guy and Allison Schmitt. You never know when your skills will call you to make a difference in the lives of others.

CHAPTER FIVE

Getting and Staying Organized

First comes the thought; then organization of that thought into ideas and plans; then transformation of those plans into reality.
—Napoleon Hill

ORGANIZATION AND EXCEPTIONAL PERFORMANCE

A football legend I've mentioned several times enjoyed twenty-two seasons of consistent NFL excellence. He won the Superbowl more times than anyone to date—seven! He's known by many as a person who's consistently dedicated to his craft and bettering himself each day, and a humble man, invested in others. He'd introduce himself to each teammate, including new drafts, and call them by name. His name? Tom Brady, NFL retiree at age forty-five (2023).

A Brady teammate and safety Devin McCourty, who played his nine-season career with the Patriots, said about Tom:

> When we played San Francisco in 2016, I want to say it was after we lost to Seattle, we had just traded Jamie Collins and we go to San Fran and I think a lot of people are doubting us and we go out and get a big win. Everybody's on the plane celebrating, standing up, laughing and joking and you look over at Tom and he's on his laptop. He got hit in the leg so he's massaging it, he's watching film and totally locked in on watching the game we just played. I think that just spoke volumes. He's always moving on to the next, he's always preparing. And that's just how he is day-in and day-out.[99]

Brady evidenced that laser-sharp focus on staying organized will generate exceptional results in any venture. Toward his elite athleticism of longevity, Brady stayed committed to a daily regimen: rising at the crack of dawn, drinking electrolyte water and a smoothie, strength and conditioning training with consistent hydration, followed by studying game footage, protein and veggies lunch, a healthy pre-practice snack, and then team practice with consistent hydration, a recovery protein shake, post-workout, healthy dinner, physical recovery work, and a 9:00 p.m. bedtime with the priority of at least eight hours sleep.[100]

Committed organization to maintain his focus and flow was fundamental to Brady leading his team to a Super Bowl victory at the unheard-of age for a quarterback, forty-three.

At age thirty-seven, Brady famously quipped: "When I suck, I'll retire. [But] I don't plan on sucking for a long time."[101] Brady's meticulous organization was fundamental to maintaining his flow and in part how he spent his career not "sucking."

Every minute detail was important to Brady for performance excellence. Even his sleep readiness and sleeping environment: no food close to bedtime, no exercise before bed, electronic devices off thirty minutes before bedtime, 65-degree temperature, dark and quiet room, bioenergetic sleepwear,[102] and high-quality mattress. It wasn't all about him, though; it was about his team and his family. His evening routine included family time and reading to his kids.[103] He showed a firm grasp on his values, which led to prioritizing, which led to organization, which led to outstanding success on and off the field.

I get it, Tom's schedule was obsessive, but he earned the finances to support the life he most wanted to live and from his passions. And that's only part of the point.

   ↝ **You don't have to be obsessive to be successful, but you do need to stay organized.**

I've experienced that people often have their financial statements scattered here, there, and everywhere, their uncoordinated assets overlapping, and little or no security to house and protect their private and personal financial documents. People are often blasé about protecting their financial paperwork (paper and digital) or they're unaware of how to keep their documentation safe.

Security doesn't have to mean that you're the one person handling all facets of your financial life, but someone of trust needs to keep your financial documents organized and secure.

   ↝ **Document organization and security are essential to peak financial fitness and success.**

I was rock climbing, my first time, with Pam and two of our three kids. My motivation behind climbing was simply the fact that I had never before rock climbed because, honestly, I was a little scared. Not scared like jumping out of a plane scared, but repelling down the face of a boulder seemed a little dangerous.

The motivation to rock climb through my fear began with a conversation with a great friend, and spiritual wellness director at Canyon Ranch, Jean Marie Mudd. She asked, "Have you ever repelled?" When I said no, she said, "Well then, I think you should! When you stick your ass over that 300-foot drop, and the only thing keeping you from falling to your death is the expert rope system and harness in front of you, there's an empowering feeling of trust. And when you release and start repelling, your confidence builds and you know you can achieve more than you thought. Letting go and trusting is empowering."

Climbing that first time, I learned that ensuring safety involves loads of rules, knots, and connectors and also having all the right tools, knowledge, and courage to take risks. I've since learned that whether a new climber or a veteran climber, those essentials don't change, and never does the logic: I may have all the right equipment, but is it organized? Am I educated in how to use each tool? If not, I'm a high-risk climber.

In that light, think of your financial house. You may have what you need—insurance, IRAs, and the rest—but if you're not organized and educated about what you have, you're at financial high risk.

My heart pounded as I squatted over a 300-foot drop. My climbing guide reassured me I was safe and everything was under control. I trusted him because of his training and experience.

Of course, those assurances and his reassurance didn't quell the river of adrenaline rushing through my veins. Although I was organized and learning the tools and rules, I needed his guidance and knew I had to trust his guidance and have faith in his expertise.

Without further thought, I leaped backward and plunged down, landing safely, both feet on the ground. I had done it! I had achieved my goal and felt exhilarated and motivated.

     ◦ **Trusting your trusted advisor can be scary but leads to amazing results and more confidence.**

That leap would not have been safe and successful had I not been committed to organization and the other principles of success I've covered that hinge on organization: knowledge gaining, practice, and expert guidance.

Picture cyclists training for the Tour De France—a prestigious annual championship. A dedicated cyclist's daily routine is getting up in the dead of night and rolling wheels long before the sun rises. The cyclist will have ensured their headgear light was charged, bike tuned, tires pumped, coffee machine timer set, water bottles filled, will have eaten a balanced dinner, laid out their riding gear, and then gone to bed for a quality time of sleep. In short, their personal organization is a well-oiled routine, fundamental to achieving their best and success.

Across all elite athletic endeavors, we see a high standard of organization. If the big game or tournament is the following day, a serious athlete isn't out the night before for dinner, drinks, and a concert. They're eating an optimal meal at the optimal time, moving through the details of their regimented routine, getting to bed at the best time, and waking up fresh, ready to move through an optimal morning routine, and hitting their sport with peak performance.

Even for golf, where raw physicality is not as important as other sports, pro golfers follow strict, well-organized routines to optimize their pre-tournament preparation and game performance. When training for a match, a pro golfer will focus on staying hydrated, getting quality sleep, working out, practicing at the range, and anything else that will benefit their game. They'll divide their training regimen to include putting, the short game, longer shots, stretching, massage, and diet. An organized routine for success.

∽ A successful financial house is a well-organized house.

Let's say your home residence is quality built and well-organized (except for your office and filing, because "nobody's going to see those"). It's 7:00 a.m., you've moved through your pristine morning routine, you're feeling charged and ready for the day and for the sweet ride sitting in your garage that will get you to work in quiet comfort.

But—your keys are missing.

You have a 9:00 a.m. meeting with a new client, preceded by a few final details that need to be tied up and followed by a busy day. But instead of that leisurely drive to the office, you're now racing around your tidy home, using colorful language, looking for your keys. You holler through the house, "Do you know where my keys are?" as if that responsibility is someone else's.

That small lack of organization just became a big deal.

By the time you found your keys (in the laundry hamper), you were pushing 7:30 and the speed limit. In your distraction and rising stress, you hit a major pothole, your left hand automatically flew from the steering wheel and your coffee from your other hand, dousing your white shirt and soaking into the carpet. In your recovery haste—well, not pretty.

You slammed into the rear end of the car ahead of you that had stopped at the red light that had been green when your car hit the hole.

In the end, you ended up with a lot of unexpected auto expenses and liability and an auto insurance policy you couldn't quickly find. Once located, you realized you weren't as familiar with your coverage as you'd thought.

A couple of kinks in your otherwise organized life cost you a heck of a lot of money and time that had to be reallocated over the next two months—time taken from work, your clients, and your golf schedule, and money from the trip you had planned.

That scenario isn't far-fetched. It's real life.

Every aspect of yourself, habits, lifestyle, and unexpected incidents are all directly tied to organization and your financial house.

Regardless of your bank balance, if you want your finances and life to flow as smoothly as possible, you need to be organized to the smallest detail— like having a designated place for your financial documents, organized and at hand.

THE JUNK DRAWER

Many of us have a junk drawer, filled with various items like batteries, paper clips, a hammer, screwdriver, tape, buttons, loose change, and pens. Likewise, almost without exception, clients consistently tell me they feel like they have a financial junk drawer—documents of bank accounts, IRAs, real estate, stocks and bonds, auto and homeowner's policies, life and health insurance, mutual funds, wills and trusts, 401(k)s, disability income protection, business ventures, and other financial documentation.

When I ask them specific questions, they typically can't give me solid answers because they're disorganized and many are unfamiliar with the details of each document.

Disorganization and unfamiliarity definitively create emotional uncertainty and insecurity and inefficiency of your time and your dollars working for you.

 Lack of control due to lack of organization and unforeseen risk factors will contribute to wealth erosion.

View the table of common personal financial documents that I discuss with my clients. As you review each item, keep these questions in mind:

> Do I know which documents I have?

> Which accounts, policies, and other financial facets do I truly need? Which ones are not best serving my lifestyle desires and future goals? And which ones need to be tweaked to better serve me?

> Which of my documents am I unfamiliar with?

> Which ones do I not fully understand and need help understanding?

FINANCIAL DOCUMENT CHECKLIST
Critical to your success in handling whatever comes your way, every financial item gets clear identificaiton and organization from one location.

INCOME
- Copy of last year's tax return

RETIREMENT
Most recent quarterly and current statements: (check all that apply)
- Company Plan (401K)
- Pension, Deferred Comp, Stock Options and Schedules
- Simplified Employee Pension (SEP)
- Individual Retirement Account (IRA)
- Annuity Statement

SAVINGS
Most recent statements from: (check all that apply)
- Bank Accounts
- Money Market Funds
- Certificate of Deposits

INVESTMENTS, BROKERAGE ACCOUNTS AND STOCK OPTIONS
- Most recent statements detailing stocks, bonds and mutual funds (including both stocks you have purchased and options you have not yet exercised)
- Crypto

REAL ESTATE
Check all that apply:
- Appraisals
- Loan Information
- Statements for your primary residence
- Statements for any vacation or investment properties

PERSONAL INSURANCE
- Schedules, premiums, benefits and lists for Disability, Long Term Care and Property & Casualty

BUSINESS OWNERSHIP
Check all that apply:
- Current balance sheets
- Current profit-and-loss statement
- Previous four years' balance sheets
- Previous four years' profit-and-loss statement
- Buyout agreements
- Business valuation/appraisal (include value of stock if publicly traded)

INHERITANCE
- Copy of trust, will or other documentation detailing your inheritance (if available; if not, and the inheritance is certain, write an amount on a note and include it)

ESTATE PLAN
- A copy of your own will, trust, or other documents detailing what you wish to be done with your assets and liabilities when you die

COLLECTIBLES
- Appraisals of current market value for precious metals, art and other collectibles

Wright Oversight & Organization

If you're a disorganized, do-it-yourselfer and you truly want to become financially fit, you must first organize your financial documents. Being organized lowers risks and increases your ability to maintain control and be prepared for the unexpected.

> Make time to organize your financial documents, which includes designating a secure place to store the paperwork.

> Dedicate time each evening to read at least one document until you have familiarized yourself with every aspect of your financial house.

> Keep a running list of written questions you need to gain answers to—whether from creditable online sources, your trusted financial advisor, or your group of financial technicians.

> Get the answers.

> Stay organized, stay on top of your budget, and the other factors of your financial house.

By the time you've spent quality time with each of your financial documents and gaining answers to your questions, you'll have a much clearer picture of your financial house, its condition (to the best of your knowledge), and how you believe it's best for you to maintain your optimal financial fitness.

Ask yourself these crucial questions and answer honestly: Will I successfully maintain peak financial organization and can I become financially fit on your own?

Some aspects of financial organization and fitness are as simple as these tasks:

> Track down your subscriptions and cancel what's unnecessary—like those forgotten online subscriptions that annually or monthly withdraw money from your bank account.

> Daily monitor and attend to your checking account activity.

> Keep your financial advisor informed of your life changes, financial changes, and goals.

If your savings (cash reserve) account is affected by spending and investments, you must frequently monitor the account(s) to make sure you're maintaining (or exceeding) your target amount.

If you're a delegator, you and your financial advisor share the responsibility of organizing, maintaining, and communicating about your financial documents.

This shared responsibility will vary by your frequency of involvement.

The delegator's relationship with their financial advisor is analogous to the relationship between an athlete and coach. If an athlete doesn't provide a coach with an accurate account of their habits, physical condition, and training, the coach cannot fully or effectively advise the athlete nor effectively use the athlete during practices and game time. For example, if an athlete doesn't inform the coach of the full extent of an injury, and plays through the pain, the athlete risks further harm, their success, and their future, and the team's chances of success.

> ∿ **The more effort and care you put into your financial organization and fitness, the greater the optimization and outcomes and the easier your life, with the payoffs of more time, more peace, and greater financial growth.**

Now consider mountaineers planning to summit Everest. Do they simply pick a date, pack some warm clothes, and hitch a ride to base camp? Not if they want to succeed.

Part of life and any venture are the unpredictable incidents (potholes) and catastrophes (pandemics) that can occur any time and place. The point of planning and preparation is not to eliminate the unexpected (impossible), but to optimize the probability of succeeding.

To succeed, the mountaineer will do everything necessary to improve their chances of success. They will be well-organized and attentive to every detail to maximize their potential and minimize risk.

CHESS AND FINANCIAL PREPAREDNESS

Chess has always been one of my favorite games. The potential to win requires skill, mastery, ability to think ahead, and strategy which require learning the game and how all the pieces work most effectively with the other pieces.

An amateur chess player may think one to three moves ahead, but a grandmaster has gained the knowledge and practiced skill to strategize fifteen or more moves ahead. Of course, every thought may not play out as planned, but here's the point: masters can make skillful predictions and wise strategies, and will organize their attacks and defense around those predictions and plans.

Unlike chess, financial rules and laws change almost yearly (taxes, for example) and so do the different techniques toward growing and protecting wealth. Most people don't have the time or interest to keep up with how these changes can detrimentally or richly affect their lives.

The best move? Partnering with a financial master or grandmaster. An expert financial advisor is well-trained and experienced in predicting, strategizing, and planning the best moves for every facet of financial success.

If you're a financial do-it-yourselfer who desires a financially fit house that has the potential to stand against opponents, you'll need to become a master. Opponents include ever-changing markets, unforeseen events, and your changing circumstances and desires.

Regardless of your approach, the checklist you reviewed on page 134 in this chapter is a key tool to help you optimize document organization.

Also important is to securely store your financial documents, paper and digital. There are a number of vault options your expert advisor can point you to.

We help to protect our clients' accounts' data through a sophisticated online tool that aggregates all their data in a secure online vault. There are many such tools available to choose from, offering similar benefits and options for document storage in a password-protected cloud account.

Paper documents like marriage license, Social Security card, and passport should be stored in a fireproof safe, either in your home or safe deposit box in your bank.

> ➤ Know exactly where all your financial information is located, including legal documents and insurance policies.

> ➤ Know exactly how much money you have in cash reserves.

> ➤ Know your total debt.

> ➤ Know your total assets.

> ➤ Have a robust process for reviewing your financial situation to ensure you're on track to fund your short-term and long-term goals.

⌇Money moves from those who do not manage it to those who do. — **Unknown**

SUMMARY

‣ Organization is essential for success in every aspect of your life. Think of yourself as a financial pro athlete in training for Olympic financial fitness.

‣ Maintaining financial organization and document security will bring you greater peace of mind, help you perform more efficiently in all areas of your life, help you more effectively achieve your financial goals, and help to free your time to enjoy the activities you desire.

‣ Organization doesn't have to be overwhelming; there are professionals at hand to assist you.

CHAPTER SIX
Benefits of a Trusted Financial Advisor

In a growth mindset, challenges are experienced as exciting rather than
threatening. So rather than thinking, oh no, I'm going to reveal my
weaknesses, you say, wow, here's a chance to grow.
— Carol Dweck

BE A TEAM PLAYER

Nick Saban was one of the greatest college football coaches ever. He recruited with a defense-first eye and won seven National championships—one with LSU (2003) and six with Alabama, the most recent in 2020.

Saban demanded the best in every situation, no complacency. He led a holistic lifestyle dedicated to habits that supported his philosophy, which he called "the process:" focusing on skills and training rather than an outcome.

In a *GQ Sports* interview titled "Nick Saban: Sympathy for the Devil," the writer referred to him as the "unsmiling, unsparing, unstoppable coach of the back-to-back national champion Alabama Crimson Tide."[104] Saban monitored everything—from how his players dressed to their body positions during sprints. *GQ Sports quoted player Barrett Jones, an offensive linesman on three of Saban's national championship teams, referring to Saban*: "He pretty much tells everybody what our philosophy is, but not everyone has the discipline to actually live out that philosophy. . . . The secret of Nick Saban is, there is no secret."[105]

Saban said of himself, "I don't think I'm complicated at all. . . . I'm not political, and I'm not trying to be diplomatic. I don't want to hurt anybody's feelings, and I don't say bad things about people. There is no agenda. There's no trying to fool somebody."[106]

Applying his approach to your financial fitness means finding a trusted financial advisor (a Saban) who's laser-focused on developing the best strategies, nailing the right investments, applying the proven techniques for saving and investing your money and implementing and monitoring the best financial plan for success, tailored to your unique needs and desires.

In team sports, any one player's performance, no matter how impressive, is less important than the team's performance. The same is true of your finances.

Equating Saban's Methods to Finances

I know an extremely successful entrepreneur. I'll call him Jason. He sold two businesses and gained more than enough money for three or four families to never again have to work. He arrived at that success by working to get better as he busted his butt and maintained a mindset of financial growth, cost trimming, and delegating.

Jason understood the benefits of delegation and had hired a team of experts in their respective fields, which helped him leverage his time to work *on* his business rather than *in* the business by hiring a president to replace him early on for one of his companies so he could focus on strategic development, and his business took off with exponential growth. He increased his multi-million robust profits by an additional $1 million in only twelve months by leveraging up and hiring that trusted advisor.

When he sold out, he again took that delegation approach by hiring our team to strategize with him to grow his personal finances because he knew the value of investing in experts. He understood the business growth sense of delegating tasks to skilled people so he could focus more on the areas he excelled in, and strengthening his balance between work and play.

Reaching and maintaining peak financial fitness for optimal success is much easier when you have skilled help, including additional resources like this book. Through previous chapters, I presented the benefits of having a trusted advisor, and now we'll look at those from the standpoint of tailoring your delegated financial plan to your unique financial needs and desires.

Look at the cockpit image of many controls and imagine yourself as a passenger on that flight. Do you need to know what the controls do? Do you need to know the variables associated with the controls? Do you even need to know how to operate any of them?

No.

You trust the pilot as well-trained, skilled, and an experienced expert. And you trust the pilot will get you safely to your desired destination in the smoothest flow possible, able to maneuver expertly around and through the elements and obstacles that appear.

Does the pilot work alone? No, he has a team on the plane and on the ground, collaborating with one purpose: to get you where you want to be while enjoying the journey.

Consider these important questions:

> Are you familiar with the ins and outs of the financial control panel that's best for your unique financial journey? For example, do you know how every trust, insurance policy, policy rider, stock, and bond works (just to name a few of many components.)

> Do you know how each of your financial components works together?

> Do you know the best time to buy and sell?

> Are you paying attention to the changing economic rules (like taxes) and economic conditions and forecasts?

> Do you know economically how to best navigate financial storms?

> Do you know how to stay ahead of the game and maintain optimal financial altitude?

If you can confidently answer yes to each, congratulations! You're either a professional financial advisor or a rare specimen. Most people are unfamiliar with the financial control panel—and you're not expected to be in the know about these things, just like you don't need to know how the inner parts of your smartphone work, or how it works with your Bluetooth. A strong current running through our daily lives is trust in our parts, pieces, equipment, technology, and the experts who make the magic happen. A friend had called it PFM—pure fucking magic.

Most clients don't care about all the details of the magic, they care about their financial destinations and having a smooth ride there without having to pilot the financial plane. They desire to reach their utmost financial dreams while doing the things they most want to do and with peace along the journey.

Returning to your flight as a passenger, imagine the pilot broadcasting, "Ladies and gentlemen, we have an 80 percent chance of landing safely." *What?!* After your initial shock, would you immediately jump from the plane?

How is that relevant to your finances? Financial plans drafted by most financial planners (technicians) have an 80 percent chance of success.

If I were to survey 100,000 people, most (if not all) would say they want a 100 percent success rate in the air—and also with their finances.

So, what's the answer?

If you're a do-it-yourselfer, there are tools and techniques, like Monte Carlo simulation (MCS), which predicts the probability of various outcomes where there are intervening variables. *ScienceDirect* defines MCS as "one of the oldest and most widely used statistical procedures for making inferences based on a small sample."[107]

Given the complexity of the modern financial landscape, it's no surprise that many collaborators and delegators consult with financial advisors. However, receiving financial advice is not the same thing as collaborating with a financial coach (advisor). You get advice from anywhere and anyone, but a true advisor brings financial expertise, focus, and accountability.

WHAT YOU SHOULD EXPECT FROM A DEDICATED TRUSTED ADVISOR:

- ➤ A close-working relationship with you to create a financial plan tailored to your particular financial needs and desires.

- ➤ Coordination and management of your financial team of respective experts.

- ➤ Team contribution of advice from their respective fields of expertise.

- ➤ Your best interest at heart; no conflicts of interest.

- ➤ Expert advice and accountability.

Just as an elite athlete benefits from their team of experts (coach, nutritionist, trainer, and other experts in varying areas), you'll benefit from a financial advisor-led team dedicated to building your wealth and helping you reach and maintain your elite financial fitness.

There are actions the team will advise you to take that you likely didn't know were important to the trajectory to achieve your goals. Think of the elite athlete coach giving action drills needed for the athlete to reach and maintain peak performance.

- ➤ Your trusted advisor should remind you of what you need to do and how and when in order to achieve your financial goals.

- ➤ Your financial advisor should help you stay on course when you wobble or you lose track of what you should be doing.

If your current independent financial technicians are not collaborating with each other and not looking at your particular bigger picture, you'll receive agenda-driven, one-size-fits-all advice instead of the best possible advice for your particular needs and goals.

Let's look at a financial advisor as a primary care doctor. When you have a medical need or you desire preventative care advice, you first go to your primary care physician. Based on your particular needs, that PCP will pull together a team of specialists because of the specialists' unique training and tools in their particular areas of expertise. For example, your primary care physician wouldn't enlist an ear, nose, and throat doctor to gain advice on your advanced Achilles tendinitis, nor your diabetes prevention diet.

Likewise, an expert in wills and trusts is not the expert in stocks and bonds. Based on your circumstances and goals, your financial advisor will

> know which specialists to pull together,

> gather their advice,

> present that expert plan to you, and

> work with you to help ensure you stay on track.

Blind Spots

When Joe Robbie, founder of the NFL Miami Dolphins football team, passed away in 1990, his family had to sell the franchise to pay over $47 million in estate taxes. If the franchise hadn't had to sell, not only could they still be the franchise owners, but at a value of over $3.2 billion at this writing.

In 2004, cosmetic entrepreneur titan and legend Estee Lauder died, and her family faced a $55 million estate tax. Fortunately, she had prior sold eleven million shares to cover the taxes.[108]

The examples show that being wealthy doesn't mean peak financial fitness. In both instances, the families could have reduced or eliminated the estate taxes with proper estate planning.

 ∾ **Anyone of any level of income who doesn't have solid financial goals and management is risking their money and their financial potential.**

Remember, the four-legged chair can't hold any amount of weight if even one leg or the seat isn't well-constructed, properly secured with the other four parts, and well-maintained.

Let's say you have a large balance in your retirement account. You've been saving for twenty or more years and have over seven figures saved. You've done everything advised through the years to maximize your retirement, including investments in the stock market. Your account has grown and is doing well, you have millions, and you're ready to retire. Sounds great! Right?

But, there's a potential problem: blind spots.

Financial blind spots are many financial risks that are not apparent to individuals who are not financial experts. Study the iceberg picture. The image shows that there are aspects of the iceberg that are seen by the naked eye and aspects hidden beneath the surface.

As we see in the image, there is

> - what we know,
> - what we don't know, and
> - the fact that what we don't know, we don't know! But, if we're talking icebergs, a glaciologist does.

The culprit of the Titanic tragedy was an iceberg, and the last bullet point—what we don't know, we don't know—is the biggest financial blind spot that can lead us into financial disaster.

If you think you don't have a blind spot, then indeed you do not know what you don't know.

For example, are you familiar with the blind spots of excise taxes on distributions from retirement funds like 401(k) and IRA? Here are a couple of current blind spot examples regarding RMDs (Required Minimum Distributions):

> For the first year following the year you reach age 72, you will generally have two required distribution dates: an April 1 withdrawal for the year you turn 72 and an additional withdrawal by December 31.[109]

Note the complexities hidden in the IRS's use of "generally." There are even blind spots in the quoted statement.

> If you don't take any distributions, or if the distributions are not large enough, you may have to pay a 50% excise tax on the amount not distributed as required.[110]

Note blind spots by IRS's general statement "not large enough." How much of your RMD is "large enough?"

The financial details you know as current facts are the parts of the iceberg you can see. Current facts and their details you don't know are your blind spots, the parts of the iceberg hidden beneath the surface.

In the late 1980s, the IRS imposed an excise tax of 15 percent on retirement plans that had what they termed "excess distributions" from qualified retirement plans. The IRS deemed excess contributions as greater than $150,000 per year. That blind spot caused a hard hit to many people's financial houses, their hard-earned money confiscated by the government before the unfair tax was repealed.

Unconscionably, the Obama administration tried to revive this additional tax levy (April 2013) on people who did the right thing, were disciplined, and saved their money! Obama proposed setting a $3 million limit on individuals' savings balances across IRAs and other tax-deferred retirement accounts. Meaning that any amount over $3,000,000 would be assessed an additional excess income tax. All of this is a potential ticking tax bomb. The example shows the danger of what is unseen beneath the surface—the part of the iceberg known by specialists. Such blind spots can wreak havoc on your retirement assets and goals. Fortunately, Obama's attempted revival didn't gain traction.

We don't know what we don't know about the threats to our financial houses—but a financial expert does.

Lingering beneath the surface are always possibilities and likelihoods of damaging tax laws and that you're not likely keeping up with such threats or the devastating changes enacted. Blind spots.

Ask your advisor if it's wise for you to follow this time-tested advice:

> ∿ **Do not put all your eggs in one basket! Take diversifying financial strategies and different types of tax-favored accounts.**

Other blind spots include

- › unnecessary accounts and accounts separated by various institutions (banking, insurance, legal, etc.) and
- › holes in the financial framework, threatening a financial collapse in part or in whole that will cause financial injuries, ruin, and even fatalities.

A trusted financial advisor will

- › know the financial blind spots and can avert you from the risks you cannot see or predict,
- › help you get your financial house in shape,
- › help you maintain optimal financial fitness that saves you time and worry,
- › focus on your unique circumstances and goals,
- › take on all the financial and administrative work with a coordinated and holistic team approach so you can focus on other things of importance to you,
- › do all the research and know the risks and options, and
- › best manage your retirement plan, investments, and all other financial aspects that you're either not interested in learning or managing or don't have the dedicated time to properly learn and manage.

Under the guidance of a trusted advisor, there can be efficiencies that help to grow profits, accelerate your goals, and enhance your peace of mind and lifestyle.

Consider the lollipop model pictured below. The client is elevated to the role of chairman of the board and the client's trusted advisor steps in to serve as the financial CEO.

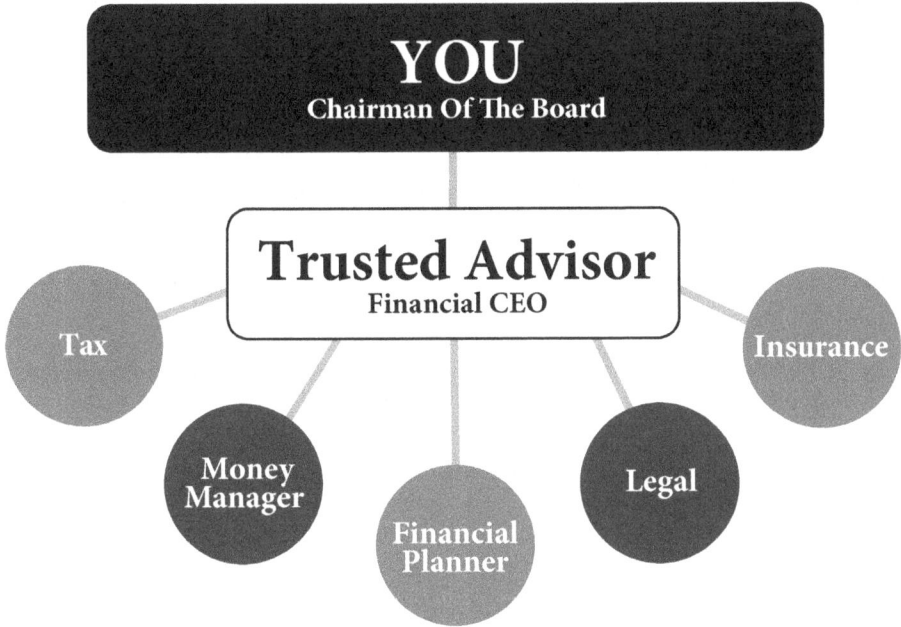

The team's approach is holistic and tailored to the client's unique circumstances and goals. The client's trusted advisor oversees the work of the team and works with the client to accomplish the client's goals.

Perhaps you're currently working with various independent technicians without an impartial team leader (trusted advisor). Your technicians may know each other but not know you're working with other technicians, and if they do, they're likely not collaborating.

Your trusted advisor should

> **coordinate** all needed financial specialists for your unique financial plan, based on your unique circumstances and goals; take a

> **comprehensive** approach, looking at everything you have, assessing what's unnecessary and what's lacking, and present you with a

- **consolidated** 'blueprint' of your customized financial house, present that financial plan, and

- **conduct** the meetings, construction, and maintenance of the plan, and

- **collaborate** with you and the team—everyone accountable.

What would it be like if your trusted advisor worked from an annual checklist of over 150 financial checkpoints that need to be addressed and confirmed for you every year? My experience is that most people don't address a fraction of the checkpoints.

Your trusted advisor can go through a comprehensive list with you to consider how many checkpoints you're attending to and completing each year, and how many are being managed by various independent technicians. Examples include:

- All debt has been reviewed, shopped, and has a specific schedule that's customized to the client's goals

- Every financial goal has a specific tactic and strategy for accumulation and decumulation, on a timeline

- Optimal asset allocation has been reviewed for every asset and confirmed that each is best positioned

- Highest yields for cash equivalents have been shopped

- All insurance has been reviewed for properties, vehicles, life, and disability insurance; the need for each has been confirmed and customized to the client's unique needs and wants

Your life becomes more simplified when your financial house is professionally designed, coordinated, consolidated, and comprehensively built and maintained. What grows is your wealth and these two invaluable commodities: your peace of mind and fun time.

Accountable is also key in any construction relationship—coach-athlete, team owner-coach, contractor-homeowner, and trusted advisor-client.

1. Your financial team is accountable to your advisor to ensure you're receiving the best and timely advice.

2. Your advisor is accountable to you for every task the team is managing

on your behalf and communicating changes and advice.

3. You're accountable to your advisor for the tasks you're handling, carrying out your advisor's advice, and communicating changes in your circumstances and goals.

The role of your trusted advisor is not to do everything *for* you but *with* you— some tasks taken by the advisor and other tasks taken by you.

Just as Nick Saban led his squads to championship after championship by getting everyone on the team into "the process" of holistic focus and flow, you will benefit from a financial coach who has a holistic process that optimizes your money working for you.

A WORD OF WARNING

There is a host of financial advisors who hold themselves as "comprehensive planners." To find a true and trusted advisor, you must follow the money and incentives that identify your prospective advisors.

▸ Your advisor's goal should be (1) unbiased and (2) focused on helping your finances perform at their elite best in peak fitness.

▸ There should be no competing incentives that motivate your advisor to prioritize advising you to buy a product for any reason other than your best interest.

▸ Therefore, you must ask prospective advisors, "How are you compensated?" If their answer presents any conflicts of interest, that advisor is not for you.

▸ Compensation policy alone does not make a trusted advisor. Find an advisor whose compensation aligns with providing you unbiased, un-incentivized, and proven advice. What's their track record?

∽ **Don't settle for less than the best.**

A trusted advisor will be

> knowledgeable of all the right questions to ask you that will create a complete picture of your current lifestyle, life circumstances, finances, and your goals in every area of your life and will ask those questions,

> skilled to move effectively and efficiently from micro and macro steps to conceptualize your customized financial plan,

> skilled in forming the best team for your peak financial fitness and goals,

> skilled in strategizing the details and quarterbacking your overall financial picture in ways that will help you make proven progress, and

> skilled in monitoring the activity and maintaining alignment with your needs and goals.

A trusted advisor's compensation will not conflict with your goals, and the advisor

> has no conflicts of interest,

> has your best interests at heart,

> will be forthcoming to discuss what is and is not in your best interest, and

> has an exhaustive list of checkpoints to best manage your financial house.

∼ It's not the job of a trusted advisor to guess what will happen in the future and hope their guesses are correct.

NOTE TO BUSINESS OWNERS
AND POTENTIAL BUSINESS OWNERS

Whether you've sold a business, still own a business, or you're considering becoming a business owner, this section may be helpful to you.

Recently, a friend—I'll call him Patrick—sold his business. The first financial technician he talked with was his investment advisor, which is sometimes a reasonable decision. The advice Patrick received? "Put all the proceeds into your investment portfolio." Patrick did.

> Remember that an investment advisor is a tradesperson. Using the house-building metaphor, an electrician, plumber, or other specialization is best overseen by the general contractor to maintain optimal flow during custom home-building.

Had Patrick first hired a trusted holistic advisor (as described previously), not just an investment advisor focused on his trade, the advisor would have known that Patrick was charitable minded and could have implemented various strategies that would have saved Patrick millions in taxes, which would have allowed him to give more to his chosen charities.

Patrick had needed a financial CEO (trusted advisor, coach, contractor) to direct him

> - prior to selling his business and
>
> - after selling his business.

Sure, eventually the advice would have included placing the funds with an investment advisor, but that's not the best first step.

TEAMWORK, NOT CONTROL

Allowing your trusted advisor and team to do what they do best doesn't mean you're giving up control, but giving up the stress and headaches of attempting to know and maneuver through all the financial laws, regulations, guidelines, blind spots, market fluctuations, and predictions—any detail you're untrained in or don't wish to manage.

> **You're the owner and your team manager is the trusted advisor you hire.**

If your bank account mirrors Nick Saban's, let your financial advisor get to work for you, doing what they do best, and trust their expertise.

If you'd rather be your own coach, a trusted advisor can help you find the financial tradespeople who will best serve for your needs.

A trusted financial advisor understands that investing in a single security or financial product, however attractive, is just a means to an end. The more important questions are:

153

> ‣ What end are you aiming for?

> ‣ What is your overall plan for reaching that destination?

An advisor who knows to ask those questions will focus on understanding your values, goals, and financial situation rather than trying to sell you a product. The advisor will help you develop a financial plan to get you from point A to point B, considering your financial resources, risk tolerance, and the time horizon.

EXERCISE

Fundamental Characteristics of Your Trusted Financial Advisor

The following are just a few of the fundamental characteristics that should be reflected in a trusted financial advisor:

‣ Ethical

‣ Insightful

‣ Leadership

‣ Experience

‣ Responsive

Considering all that you've learned, add the additional character traits that are important to you in a financial advisor:

‣ _____

‣ _____

‣ _____

‣ _____

‣ _____

‣ _____

‣ _____

‣ _____

Ask yourself:

> - Does my financial or investment advisor do the things mentioned above?
>
> - How would I describe my financial advisor?
>
> - Am I just settling because the advisor hasn't done something terribly wrong, and it's a pain in the ass to concern myself with the details?

As you interview financial advisors, there are other signs that will let you know if you're in safe hands. Here's one: the advisor will interview you to determine if they want to work with you. Their questions will help them have a working knowledge of

> - the extent of financial help you need,
>
> - your mindset regarding your level of involvement—to what degree you're willing to delegate financial tasks and take instructions.
>
> - your goals and your level of motivation to reach your goals.

~ Winning is not complicated. People complicate it. If you surround yourself with the right people, you win.[111] — **Dick Vermeil**

Once you've chosen your trusted advisor, you'll be expected to trust and follow their recommendations.

When Nick Saban showed up as head football coach, did the players question his advice like, "But how is that going to work?" Or did they trust him and get on with it?

Saban was there to lead the players to victory and expected his goal was also the goal of his players. He was the trusted advisor. Likewise, your advisor will expect you and every member of your financial team to have the same goal and commitment: to get your financial house in order, achieve peak financial fitness, and stay fit.

GREAT FINANCIAL COACHES AND NAVY SEAL TRAINING

I heard Peyton Manning, NFL great and Hall of Famer, speak at an annual Waste Management kick-off lunch in Phoenix, Arizona. The experience reinforced in me that even the greatest athletes continue to lean on their coaches to achieve better results.

Manning talked about the major impact coaches had on him and that even after many years in the league as an all-star quarterback, he'd return each summer to see his former quarterback coach, David Cutcliffe.

Coach Cutcliffe had drilled in him to keep going back to the basics, including fundamentals like taking a snap or calling a play in the huddle. Why did Cutcliffe do that, even after Manning had played in the NFL for over a decade? Manning explained that the little things matter, and that if we think otherwise, in whatever job we're doing, that's when we need to worry about our game sliding.

In finance, the same point holds true. While the financial market constantly changes, there are time-tested principles that apply to investing long term. If you forget the basics, stray from the fundamentals of risk management, the result can be a costly lesson in market behavior. A trusted advisor will be well-equipped to help you avoid such mistakes, keep you focused on the fundamental principles of investing, and make sure you remain open to *investigating* new trends and opportunities.

    ∿ A trusted advisor will have earned a degree in finance and achieved certifications from various training programs.

Such training challenges and better equips the advisor to become the best.

To improve my ability to offer my clients the best service possible, I attended what I consider to be the financial equivalent of Navy Seal training. Think of it like Sandboxx described:

> Other than being as tough as nails, Navy SEALS have to meet quite a few other requirements when it comes to the rigorous Navy SEAL training program.

> And not all who apply for the job make it — even Olympic athletes have tried and failed.[112]

The extensive financial program I entered encompassed four years of quarterly training in brutal six-and-half-day sessions. Participants were hand-picked from around the world by financial instructor Bill Bachrach, an acclaimed author, Hall-of-Fame keynote speaker, and financial *sensei* and coach. Participants came from Australia, the UK, the Netherlands, and from across the United States.

All told, the annual per-person training cost was similar to the annual tuition of an Ivy League school. When I started attending the program in 2015, the total room, board, tuition, etc. at Harvard was $58,607. My tuition for the program was $60,000 per year for four years. A serious venture for serious, proven financial advisors.

Every attendee was a twenty-plus-year finance veteran in their respective financial specialties. Participants included CPAs, attorneys, investment advisors, and insurance specialists—each an elite technician.

But our credentials and experiences were not why we were there.

Akin to Navy Seal candidates, we were there to become the best of the best, to grow even stronger in leadership skills by taking challenges that were greater than any we'd faced in our careers. The financial training was more taxing than the Ironman challenges I had faced.

The training featured various requirements, including recorded meetings we listened and studied like football players and coaches study NFL game film.

Bill reviewed and coached us to not only improve our communication skills but to deliver the best elite service possible to high-achieving families. The goal? Delivering on the promise to clients that we would get their financial houses in pristine order and keep them in peak financial fitness. A monumental task. Like Navy Seal candidates, several financial elitists tapped out because of the training's demands.

During those four years, I missed a lot of family events, but I was determined (like every challenge I undertake) to reach my potential by exceeding what I thought were my limitations.

It's been said that 10,000 hours are required to become an expert at something, but I believe that theory needs to be rephrased: we must practice doing things correctly, most effectively, for many hours to achieve our best. Doing shit, half-ass work, for 10,000 hours is 10,000 hours of shit. But 10,000 hours of specific, purposed work, done at an exceptional level, yields amazing outcomes with enormous positive impact.

Now, imagine practicing a tennis serve with the wrong technique for 10,000 hours. You'll perfect an ineffective or less-effective serve. Practicing a proven technique will prove more effective. A master tennis coach will ensure you're not only serving well but winning matches.

Likewise, if you apply proven financial principles and techniques advised by your trusted advisor, you'll achieve peak financial fitness.

SUMMARY

> - A trusted advisor's job in overview is to

>   1. work with you to develop your custom financial plan so you'll have the highest probability of achieving your goals, regardless of what happens in the market, economy, or the world at large.

>   2. implement the plan and advise you on adjustments as you stick to the plan, no matter what happens outside of your control.

> - Find a trusted advisor who has your best interests at heart—no conflicts of interest.

> - Know that you have blind spots, learn those from your financial expert and how to best handle each.

> - Stay in communication with your trusted advisor and follow the advisor's recommendations to help ensure you will reach your financial goals and maintain peak financial fitness.

CHAPTER SEVEN
Embracing the Practice Grind

Some people dream of success
while others wake up and work hard at it.
—Unknown

THE GRIND

Olympian Michael Phelps had natural gifts and a body perfectly proportioned for swimming. He's well known for his single-minded dedication to practice and overall fitness (eating right, thinking right, sleeping right), which enabled him to win the most Olympic medals of any athlete in history to date (2023)— 28 total with 23 gold—and he broke 39 world records.[113] In the 2008 Beijing Olympics, Phelps's best achievement was a record-breaking 8 gold medals.[114] According to the *New York Times*, Phelps "lived for the races."[115]

He's another prime example of an athlete who adhered to a strict and holistic routine, embracing grinding practices to maximize his ability to compete well in every event. He'd rise at 6:00 a.m. and swim for two hours. Then he'd weight train for an hour. Imagine having done three hours of exercise every day by 10:00 a.m.

Phelps trained so intensely, he had to eat between 6,000 and 8,000 calories a day[116] for the energy to maintain his strength and training.

To keep pace in the grind, he lived by this principle: "If you put a limit on anything, you put a limit on how far you can go. I don't think anything is too high. The more you use your imagination, the faster you go. If you think about doing the unthinkable, you can."[117] He kept winning because his mindset was in the grind.

Grinding practice in finances can also pay huge dividends. As tennis legend Chris Evert said, "Wherever you set your sights, . . . be proud of every day that you are able to work in that direction."[118]

~ Talent without work is nothing.[119] —Christiano Ronaldo

We've looked at several elite athletes who are legendary for their superhuman dedication to practice, not just before competitions but afterward. You won't see peak performers settling; they're always pushing and growing with a mindset on the grind and success.

The same mindset, embracing the practice grind, applies optimal financial fitness. Did you know that your financial health directly affects your physical and mental health?

> A nationwide survey of more than 3,000 adults published by Thrive Global and the credit card Discover in March 2022, found that 90 percent reported that money was a source of stress.

> About two-thirds of respondents reported feeling like they can't overcome the financial difficulties that are piling up, and 40 percent reported taking no steps to secure their financial future.[120]

If you aren't actively protecting your wealth by embracing the practice grind, you're putting your hard-earned money and your physical and mental health at risk. The number of people cavalier about both is staggering, which frightens me as a finance expert. I've witnessed people's financial health decline and fatalities—all of which were preventable.

GROWING BETTER WITH PRACTICE
AND KNOWLEDGE-GAINING

Whether you're poor at sports, in health, or in wealth, you can grow better by setting your mind to practice the grind and by consistently practicing and growing your mind by learning and using the best

> ➤ techniques,

> ➤ tools, and

> ➤ team.

You don't need to learn every detail there is to know about holistic health and fitness to live life in a healthy grind, although you will need to commit to ongoing learning from experts. Mike Rayburn Leonard, Hall of Fame speaker, guitar player, and humorist, said, "It's not about being good at everything; it's about being GREAT at the most important things. Coasting only happens downhill."[121]

His statement illustrates a major theme we've been exploring in this book: You don't need to master the knowledge of every element of financial planning and maintenance to achieve your financial goals. Regardless of the degree you collaborate with financial experts and learn from other trusted financial sources, the goal is the same:

    ~ **Ensure your finances are daily improving regardless of what challenges appear in the world and within your life.**

Unless you're among the micro percentage of people born into great wealth or you've won the Mega Millions jackpot, you must consistently practice hard and smart to reach your goals, financial and otherwise, and maintain fitness. Sure, you'll have pockets of luck from time to time, but as they say, *you gotta make your own luck.*

In any aspect, successful people allocate time to improve their smarts to be more effective and efficient in their practices. They talk with experts and they read, listen to, and watch educational information presented by experts. They spend time in enlightening conversations with successful people, learning, masterminding, and applying the knowledge in their daily grind.

Remember me saying that you should spend time daily in your finances? Every day offers us opportunities to learn something new, like better understanding investing and discovering more income streams. The more you treat your finances as a significant and fundamental part of your whole-health quality, the healthier and more fit your financial house will be.

    ~ **Regardless of goals, successful people continue to grow.**

By embracing the practice grind, successful people achieve and maintain a fit financial house, strongly rooted in values and wise principles and structured to withstand whatever adversity shows up. They practice hard and smart using the best (1) techniques, (2) tools, and (3) team. The outcome is growth in savings and investments, enabling them to reach and exceed their financial and lifestyle objectives.

If there's anything you must take from this chapter, it's this: Ideally, hire a trusted advisor. If you're not yet able to afford an advisor, work toward that while spending daily time in your finances—monitoring, learning, and practicing. An elite financial house is 10 out of 10.

Reaching and maintaining elite financial health and fitness (like anything else) is not a one-and-done attempt but a *lifestyle* of ongoing practice, embracing the grind, whether you're a do-it-yourselfer or you have a trusted advisor and team.

SETBACKS

Setbacks are an inevitable part of life—but a setback is far different from a defeat.

> ➤ Setback is defined as: a checking of progress[122]

> ➤ Defeat is defined as: obsolete: DESTROY[123]

Remembering the difference whenever you have a setback will make all the difference in your success.

> *If you're trying to achieve, there will be roadblocks. I've had them; everybody has had them. But obstacles don't have to stop you. If you run into a wall, don't turn around and give up. Figure out how to climb it, go through it, or work around it.[124]* —**Michael Jordan**

Your investments, for example, will not perform well 100 percent of the time. Unanticipated expenses, changes in employment, and market fluctuations may also adversely affect your finances. Regardless, when you stay true to embracing the grind, your chances of overcoming setbacks, avoiding defeats, and becoming financially elite are substantially greater.

STAMINA

An athlete's physical and mental stamina is as important as their speed, strength, and technique. In positioning, for example, an athlete's fatigue diminishes awareness of factors, remembering strategies, and making and executing rapid decisions.

Staying in peak physical fitness directly helps your cognitive fitness, maximizing your ability to make smart decisions and keep up the productive grind in every area of your life. Regarding your finances, when you're mentally, physically, and financially fit, the natural outcome is not only monetary but greater enjoyment of your money.

Increased Lifespan

According to studies, staying financially fit may affect your lifespan. For example, Harvard was reported to have analyzed "1.4 billion Internal Revenue Service records on income and life expectancy." The results showed "staggering differences in life expectancy between the richest and poorest" and "evidence that low-income residents in wealthy areas, such as New York City and San Francisco, have life expectancies significantly longer than those in poorer regions."[125]

So get out there and daily exercise your body and mind, and stay on top of your financial fitness.

Summary

> ‣ The grind intersects with every area of your life. Embracing the grind today increases the probability of richer and fuller tomorrows.

> ‣ Every day, learn something new about finances.

> ‣ Practice increases profit in every area of your life: physical, mental, emotional, spiritual, financial, and even lifespan.

CHAPTER EIGHT
Taxes, Inflation, Investments, and The Case for Hiring

The quality of a man's life is in direct proportion to their commitment to excellence, regardless of their chosen field of endeavor.
—Vince Lombardi

Owners of sports franchises are not typically the best choice for selecting players, much less picking the plays. An owner's skills are usually in other business areas and a wise owner will find a skilled general manager and coach to run the team.

> "Charlie-O"—Charles Finley, longtime owner of the Oakland A's—is an example of a quasi-collaborator in a do-it-yourself jumpsuit, both as an owner and with his finances. *ESPN* reported that Finley's twenty-year ownership was "one of the most erratic administrations in baseball history."[126] Franz Lidz, *Sports Illustrated*, interviewed "the ever-combative Finley" twelve years after the owner sold the team. Lidz wrote, "Acting as his own general manager, head scout and business manager, Finley hired and fired . . . 25 broadcasters, 10 farm directors and 17 managers."[127]

As for Finley's financial house, he sold the team in 1980 and told *The Washington Post*, "I'm almost bankrupt, but not yet," referencing the $12.7 million sale that would be eaten up by his staggering medical bills from tuberculosis. Finley had become wealthy from his insurance empire that offered group disability to physicians and profited Finley $20 million annually from over 70,000 doctors. [128] Oddly though, he didn't have his own insurance.[129]

ESPN also reported that in Finley's post-baseball years, he suffered several business setbacks and lost much of his fortune.[130]

Unlike Finley, you may be pretty skilled as the general manager of your money. But, let's look at the complexities of taxes, inflation, and investments.

➤ **Income Tax**—An unfortunate reality is that a significant part of our income will go to taxes. Are you doing everything in your power to ensure your tax burden is as low as possible? Your certified public accountant, looking at your financials, can tell you how much you made last year and how much you owe the government. But are their calculations correct? How do you know? Have you had their work checked? And did they provide you with strategies to reduce your taxes or did they just tell you how much you owed?

Given the significant impact taxes can have on your income and overall net worth, taking a comprehensive approach to optimize (decrease) your tax burden is significant to financial fitness.

That perfect 10 financial score you're aiming for is impossible without optimizing your taxes.

Your trusted advisor should have the network to steer you to a skilled and trusted CPA or enrolled agent to ensure the best advice on income tax. If not, that's a sign to steer yourself to a different advisor. If you're a do-it-yourselfer, you'll want to dive into researching income tax laws to prevent losing a lot of money unnecessarily.

➤ **Estate Taxes**—A financially fit house isn't just about your lifetime. Financial decisions affect your family members after your death. The right advice or research will help your family avoid post-death issues, such as not having the right trust(s), to save your estate from being swallowed up to 50 percent piecemeal by Uncle Sam. We're not guaranteed a tomorrow, so set up your trusts now, if you haven't already, and ensure the trusts remain fit.

To those who are wealthy: Under federal tax law at this writing (2023), a married couple's estate valued at $24.12 million or more is subject to estate taxes. To avoid a high tax burden and save your hard-earned money and other assets (businesses, estates, farms, etc.) on gift tax, there are a variety of sophisticated techniques and strategies to take— like CLATs, CRUTs, and GRATs. Ask your trusted advisor or research estate and gift tax laws for protective strategies.

To the rest of us (net worths under $25 million): Establishing trusts or LLCs can help protect your assets from taxation, lawsuits, and creditors. Unfortunately, we live in a litigious society, and protecting our assets has become even more important. Don't put this off any longer. The time is now.

Having the right legal advisor for trusts or LLCs is essential, especially if you're buying rental property or starting a business with a partner. An alternative to hiring a legal advisor is creating an inexpensive revokable living trust online.

Why trusts are important: Over the years, I come across multiple people who sold their businesses and put the profits with an investment advisor. The technician was happy and appreciative because—DING!—that's how they earn their revenue. Missing from these transactions were *gift trusts*, which would have saved or eliminated millions of dollars in taxation. The individuals had blind spots, not knowing what they didn't know in hand with a lack of coordination among these sellers' independent financial technicians. Technicians may have motivation from their area of expertise, but that's not always in concert with the others. Instead of unnecessarily gifting Uncle Sam with a bonus, those excess dollars could have gone to philanthropic causes, for example.

A trusted advisor would have shown the individuals the bigger picture and implemented tax-saving strategies. Lack of tactical planning is avoidable.

▸ **Inflation as Tax**—As of 2022, inflation rose to the highest in decades and had the government printing more money. Inflation is another hidden tax that creates huge financial burdens in society. Examples include rising interest rates and businesses forced to drive up prices because consumers buy less. Inflation can cause widespread devastation, not just financially. The burden of inflation also weighs on us mentally and emotionally, which negatively affects physical health.

As the investor, you're the owner of your portfolio. Your hired advisor is the head coach who manages your investment portfolio. You won't fire yourself and, of course, neither will your advisor likely fire you. So, trust and respect are essential between the investor and advisor.

Except for the likes of Charlie-O, even the most hands-on sports team owners know the value of hiring a head coach and refraining from trying to coach and manage their teams. A team owner trusts the head coach's training, skills, and experience. Even before sports franchises became billion-dollar assets, what was clear to team owners was that on-the-field coaching was best assigned to those with expertise who would also be invested in the job's day-to-day grind, sharing the same goals: to strategize and make crucial decisions about plays and players, to motivate and inspire optimum performance, developing a winning team.

A trusted advisor is aware of vulnerabilities, like investments in CDs, bonds, money markets, and savings accounts. While such investments can help to protect your money from stock market volatility to some degree, they may not keep pace with inflation.

Some of the more conservative investment choices, like bonds, pose interest rate risk as bonds are sensitive to rate changes. Therefore, much of the total return comes from income, which is predetermined (for most bonds), hence the term "fixed income." As inflation rises, fixed income delivered by bonds is worthless. If you're not careful, even the safest types of investments can have negative consequences in the long run.

Investors who have long-term investment goals but invest in safer investments may have a difficult time keeping pace with inflation and lower interest modes.

> **Recall Inflation: "I caught a 40-pound bass!"**

Multiple studies found that investors have a habit of remembering their returns as bigger than they actually were—like the fisherman's greatest catch grows larger with each retelling.

Financial investments can reap big results and recall inflation, which can be financially self-sabotaging for the do-it-yourselfer (and those who haven't done their homework before hiring a financial advisor).

Inflated recall leads to:

- overconfidence,

- higher trading frequency, and

- loss of wealth.

Studies invariably confirm that most stock traders lose money in the short term, and almost all traders lose in the long term:

- A study of eToro users found that about 80% active on the platform lose money, with an average return of -36.3% over 12 months.

- A Brazilian study found that 97% of individuals who day trade for more than 300 consecutive days lose money, and only 1.1% earn more than the Brazilian minimum wage.

- A Securities and Exchange Commission (SEC) study found that 70% of foreign exchange traders lose money every quarter, and on average 100% of a retail customer's investment is gone within 12 months.

- A study of Robinhood users finds that the platform encourages the trading of stocks with the most outsized positive or negative returns, and the top 0.5% of stocks bought each day loses 4.7% over the following month as a result.[131]

> **Investment Selection**

Nick Saban's well-known athlete selecting process included consistent time in watching the performances of potential high school recruits. This focused attention to performance details enabled him to best determine which athletes were more likely to be winning investments for his team.

Likewise, your advisor will watch the performance of financial products over time to determine which ones consistently create above-average returns. The results can be astonishing. Considering the power of compounding earnings means that if your investments perform poorly, you are likely leaving significant sums of money on the table.

A dedicated, trusted advisor with no conflicts of interest will take the dedicated studying approach—delving deeply into researching, watching potential investments, evaluating the fit for your particular financial goals, and creating an investment portfolio for your consideration.

> **Portfolio Management**

In sports, a team's success in part depends on the coach's management skills during games—knowing what player to put in and pull out, when, and what plays to call.

Likewise, an elite, trusted advisor stays in the grind and knows which investment category or class performs best during various economic conditions. Their research and evaluations will include looking at insurance, tax, legal, advance-planning techniques, staying up to date on the latest and best software, and switching investment managers when necessary—like the head coach of a winning pro team will substitute players based on their performances. Such an advisor is in the best position to advise you on investment strategies.

The expert advisor knows the different asset classes, which may perform better or worse in various market conditions. The expert's work includes

- monitoring market fluctuations, taking a long-term approach,

- monitoring your portfolio's asset allocation to be aware of needed changes that will strive to optimize your returns, and

- rebalancing your portfolio as needed in response to composition changes brought on by market performance, or changes in your investment objectives.

As for composition changes due to market performance is this example: when one sector of the market does very well, your portfolio may be over-invested in that sector, calling for rebalancing to align your holdings with recommended allocation.

As for changes in your investment objectives, a common scenario is that your risk tolerance decreases as you near or enter retirement. Why? Because at that stage of life, there's less time to make up for a big portfolio drawdown if there's a bear market (declining market values). Also, retirees are less inclined to invest as aggressively as they might have when younger.

So your critical part in portfolio management is communicating to your advisor any changes in your life circumstances and financial goals.

THE MEANS TO PEAK FINANCIAL FITNESS

By this point in your reading, you get the importance of your role and the role a trusted advisor can play in ensuring your financial house is in order, reaching peak financial fitness, and staying on top, your money working for you rather than you working for your money.

However, you may be saying, "I want a trusted advisor, but I don't have the means to hire one."

There's a complex process in making the decisions necessary to optimize your investments, save money on taxation, and protect your financial house in times of inflation and other economic pitfalls and disasters. In order to reach peak financial fitness and objectives, the process requires extensive training, experience, and focused dedication in the grind. Considering these factors, the answer to the question, "Do I need a financial advisor?" the answer is yes;—find an expert who has your best interests at heart—no bias, no conflicts of interests, fully dedicated and proven. Start looking, and use the guidelines of this book, including the following.

KNOW YOUR INVESTMENT PHILOSOPHY

Sports team owners will look for a manager who has a similar philosophy about what it takes to win. Likewise, you should know your investment philosophy and the approach of your potential financial advisor before hiring to manage your investments. If you've already hired an advisor, do you know their approach? Have you determined how fitting their philosophy is with yours?

Ask yourself these questions:

- ➤ What are my investment goals?

- ➤ What is my investment approach?

- ➤ How is the advisor compensated?

- ➤ Does their compensation present any conflicts to my best interests?

- ➤ If not,

- ➤ how similar is the advisor's investment philosophy to mine?

  - • If comparable, are the similarities an optimal fit for my financial goals?

  - • If different, can the advisor make a strong case for changing my approach?

The answers will help you determine whether the advisor is right for you. After all, it's your money, life, and legacy. So, ensure you're comfortable with an advisor before hiring.

The modern investment climate is volatile, even when the market is rising. There are often sectors of the economy and market that may not do as well. As a result, significant expertise and due diligence are required to preserve and grow your wealth.

Are you qualified to handle this task yourself?

Chances are, like the owner of a pro sports team, no matter how successful and smart you are, you're better off finding a trusted advisor who shares your overall investment philosophy and is devoted to the day-to-day work of building, monitoring, and managing your investment portfolio for you.

Summary

> Pay attention to your taxes and tax laws, as a trusted advisor would, to ensure you're not paying the government more than necessary.

> Inflation and other such market effects are part of life, so stay on top of the factors and fluctuations and stay smart in your decisions.

> Investments are never free of risk, but there are things you can do to ensure you're thinking long term.

> Speak to your trusted advisor about the best investment portfolio for your goals.

> Know your financial philosophy, discuss that with your trusted advisor to ensure you both see eye-to-eye; and if you don't have an advisor yet, seek one.

CHAPTER NINE
Innovation, Trends, and
the Brave New World of Cryptocurrency

Talent is cheaper than table salt. What separates
the talented individual from the successful one is a lot of hard work.
— Stephen King (paraphrased)

"The Rock" and Crypto

A significant part of pro wrestling is the extravagant characters wrestlers play in the ring and in the media, which is how they get the crowds going. There's the hero, known as a "face," and the villain, known as a "heel."

Former pro wrestler Dwyane "The Rock" Johnson, coiner of the term "smackdown," became famous as a face and known for his wrestling moves "The Rock Bottom"[132] and "The People's Elbow."[133] His charismatic jovial arrogance eventually pulled wrestling fans to his side, and he rose to fame and fortune and rode well through the rises and falls. What set The Rock apart was not only his innovation but his years in the grind of consistent hard work.

Financial investment innovations and trends are characters vying for attention. The newest one in the ring and working hard to be seen are cryptocurrencies, like the famous Bitcoin. If you're not yet informed about crypto, it's digital currency and Bitcoin is currently the most well-known digital coin in the ring.

Cryptocurrency was introduced in 2008 and is now in our mainstream market. The defining difference between our US dollars and crypto is that digital dollars have no centralized authority (no financial institution).

Ringside and keenly watching the crypto characters are prominent investors with divided views. Some have assessed digital currencies as rising heroes and others as investor smackdowns. An article by *U.S. News & World Report* exampled the two camps, some viewing Bitcoin as a face and others as a heel. "In 2013, Forbes named Bitcoin (BTC) the year's best investment. In 2014, Bloomberg countered with its proclamation of Bitcoin being the year's worst investment.[134]

Multi-billionaire Warren Buffet described crypto in 2018 as "a gambling token"[135] and in 2023, when asked by CNBC to comment on Charlie Munger's statement, "Bitcoin's like rat poison." Buffet replied, "Well, it's probably more like--rat poison squared."[136]

Among a host of other ringside critics are Nobel prize-winning economist Paul Krugman and Microsoft founder Bill Gates.[137] On the other side are crypto enthusiasts like Carolina Panthers' Russell Okung, the first NFL athlete to be paid in Bitcoin.[138] He tweeted in December 2020, "When we are all paid in Bitcoin, no one can tell us what to do with the value we create."[139]

A month later, January 2021, *CoinDesk* reported that cryptocurrency's market value had hit a record $1 trillion.[140] A year later, they reported that billionaire investor Bill Miller invested 50 percent of his personal wealth in Bitcoin, calling the cryptocurrency "digital gold"[141] and advised people to put 1 percent of their money in the current-reigning crypto champion.

While investors have opposing views, what each of the mentioned influencers has in common is innovation, keeping their eyes on innovations and trends, and dedicating decades of hard work to their respective innovative passions.

Why is the subject of crypto important to the rest of us?

Digital assets will probably eventually usurp traditional paper money. Skeptical? There was a time, in the not-so-distant past, when the majority wasn't buying the idea that man would make it to the moon, much less plant our flag in its soil.

There's also the computer innovation. Who knew that the worldwide web would become the prime human and AI connection of communication and completing tasks that have become digitized?

The reported success of cryptocurrencies proves the need for us to stay aware of this new technology and other progressive ideas and trends to remain well-informed of our options. As we're forced by the power of change into this new world trading means, we must stay well-informed of the trajectory of the market.

The point is to ensure our financial houses remain in peak fitness as technology pioneers ahead.

ᗌ **Diversity and keeping up with financial trends are key. Be wise to learn more about cryptocurrency.**

Like market fluctuation, "The Rock" Johnson repeatedly flipped from face to heel, back and forth from 1997 to 2013 as an outstanding athlete with a knack for character in the ring and on the microphone. Within just two years of joining the WWF (now WWE), he won the Intercontinental title. The WWF storyline turned Rocky Maivia into "The Rock" as a heel, he rapidly grew in popularity as he captured several titles in 1998. From 2004 to 2013, The Rock was sensationalized as a face and became known as the face of WWE. His fame reached well beyond sports. He became internationally famous as a feature films star, producer, entrepreneur, philanthropist, inspirational speaker . . . and co-owner of Xtreme Football League.

ᗌ **Skill is only developed by hours and hours of work. —Unknown**

The Rock didn't become a multi-million-dollar success on his own. He relied on teams of experts in their respective fields as he moved into and became accomplished in varying ventures. Besides winning 17 WWF titles, Johnson's celebrity grew broader when he debuted as a villain in the movie *The Mummy Returns* (2001). His $5.5M paycheck for playing the leading role of *The Scorpion King* made the Guinness Book of World Records as the highest paid actor for a debut leading role.[142]

Johnson stayed in the grind and his legacy as a face is here to stay.

Where will cryptocurrency ultimately land? Face or heel?

We don't know. What we know is that research and watching products and their performance are paramount to planning the portfolio holder's future.

ᗌ ***Don't leave your portfolio to chance; follow the advice of your trusted advisor.***

Whether you view cryptocurrency as a face or heel, the subject is increasingly relevant to your financial house. Like The Rock's rise to fame, cryptocurrency continues to grow in prominence and may very well become part of your investment portfolio.

Crypto was invented in 2008, having a value of zero dollars. Soon after, the first exchange took place for less than a tenth of a cent per Bitcoin. At this writing, fifteen years later, a Bitcoin is worth a staggering $27,861.[143]

What's the evidence of crypto' rise?

As of June 7, 2023, the current market capitalization was $44.42 billion.[144] By comparison, Ford Motor Company, a giant wrestler in the economy ring since 1903 had a market cap of $54.11 billion.[145]

What Can We Learn from Sports Innovations and Trends?

Fierce competition in the sports ring has led to a technological and fitness arms race. Elite athletes are going to great lengths to keep an edge over their competition. An edge can prove the difference between the fine line of winning and losing. To help athletes maintain peak performance, their sport experts stay on top of the latest research and technologies. For example, the cold plunge method for tissue repair, muscle pain, and swelling has advanced to the now-popular cryotherapy.

This is true of trusted advisors. They know the latest technologies, trends, and best strategies and options available to you. They know what's happening with crypto.

The more you know about innovations and trends, the better decisions you'll make to create and maintain peak financial fitness.

Golf is a good example of staying on top of trends. Back in the day, golfers smoked while playing and otherwise paid little attention to their overall fitness. Aside from playing and practicing shots on the links and putts in their offices, the sport didn't demand much physical excellence.

This changed in 2006 with the fitness evolution. Most golf pros have since adopted detailed nutrition plans, some going so far as tailoring meal planning to their gut biome and gene type! Competition has grown fiercer with the rise of professional golfers. One golfer gaining an edge from new techniques and technology motivates other golfers to do the same. So, pros typically engage in comprehensive, innovative stretching and training routines, like the method TPI (Titleist Performance Institute), and other steps that optimize physical and mental fitness.

How does this apply to your finances?

New financial technologies and trends have a major impact on the fairway of investments. Just as a golfer and his caddie will scout out the lay of the course and its hazards, the job of a trusted advisor is to know and continually evaluate the financial landscape. The advisor will look at every factor to determine how those may positively and negatively affect your financial planning and goals.

CRYPTO CAUTION

An initial appeal of digital dollars revolved around the idea that cryptocurrency would protect people from inflation. How? By serving as inflation hedges—restricting issuance of cryptocurrency to a specified number of units, as with Bitcoin.

But that idea hasn't turned out to be true.

The argument is that out-of-control printing of fiat currency (like the US dollar) will increase the relative value of limited, circulating cryptocurrency. Bitcoin is capped at $21 million coins—no more to be created and unknown whether that cap will ever be reached. The cap makes Bitcoin finite, unlike gold, which can still be mined.

The success of Bitcoin and other cryptocurrencies is yet unknown. In the long run, the current level of popularity among investors shows that the concept of a non-fiat value source can generate significant interest among investors for portfolio diversification.

However, regulations for digital currencies are not the same as those for fiat money.

~ **Investors must understand the legal aspects of crypto to avoid smackdowns.**

For example, at this writing, the US classifies cryptocurrency as *property*. This means you, as an investor in crypto, will have to follow the law about *capital gains* when filing your taxes. You're wise to consult a tax accountant who's familiar with digital currencies.

With no central agency controlling cryptocurrency, supporters highlight this decentralization as a benefit. This benefit can be financially liberating, as long as digital money isn't subjected to the restrictions and regulations on fiat currency. But crypto has serious legal challenges. Here's a good example: With no central authority for investors to turn to when problems arise—like crypto fraud—investors can face enormous legal challenges. Currently, the most common legal issue is cryptocurrency fraud.

Legal recourse has just recently emerged for victims of crypto fraud. In mid-2022, California became the first state to apply the "unfair and deceptive acts or practices law" to fraudulent cryptocurrency exchanges."[146]

~ **When a crypto "heel" scams a crypto "face," the victim may not have legal recourse.**

For every successfully emerging technology company, there are folding companies, losing the money of their owners, funders, and public investors. This loss doesn't even consider the scamming that's often perpetrated by unscrupulous individuals taking advantage of a hot investment sector. A good example, the cryptocurrency Squid, inspired by the popular TV show *Squid Game*. When the currency creators (unknown) scammed investors in a rug pull, the smackdown cost investors a loss of $2.1 million.[147]

~ **Anyone investing or considering investment in cryptocurrency should familiarize themselves with the legal aspects and how digital currencies are taxed.**

Will cryptocurrencies usher in fundamental changes in the way people live their lives?

Likely. As with any broad-span technology.

We know that digital currencies have certainly had a significant impact from an investment and utility standpoint. The value of digital dollars has skyrocketed. The ability to easily blockchain transactions with parties around the globe has made this new technology attractive.

China has banned cryptocurrency since 2013. The US, however, remains focused (at this writing) on developing regulations to protect crypto investors in securities (such as stocks and bonds). While we don't know what this focus will ultimately mean for cryptocurrency investors, the attention suggests that cryptocurrencies will continue to be available for investment, at least in the short run.

Tremendous profits from Bitcoin for early investors remind us that those who identify new trends can benefit from pioneers' insight. Predicting trends of this type is easier said than done, and investments in future technologies are often highly speculative.

My point is not to change your investing style or risk tolerance in favor of jumping on the latest trend. My point is to urge you to stay knowledgeable about new innovations and trends. Product and trending knowledge will help you determine if it's wise to dedicate a portion of your risk-oriented asset allocation.

> ～ **A cautious approach to new and trending investment opportunities is always wise and worthy of the advice of a trusted investment manager.**

A trusted advisor will know who's in the ring, what's happening, and which "faces" are safest to bet on.

Part of being cautious is to ask yourself these "back to the basics" questions:

- ▸ What are the current big and best trends?

- ▸ How can I stay in the know about new innovations?

- ▸ Who can help me stay in the know about which innovations are proving to be a heel or a face and will best advise me?

Surveying the past century, we see the technologies that have made money and lost money for investors. A prime example is the 1830s' innovative and quickly trending railroad revolution. And the "financial panic of 1973"[148]when a mass number of railroads fell into bankruptcy. But ultimately, trains became a commonplace means of daily commuting, extensive traveling, and distribution.

Now consider the internet and technology stocks of the 1990s that reached tremendous valuations before crashing in 2000. While many dot.com stocks bombed, several that survived never regained their peak. Others took many years just to regain their financial footing.

The price of Bitcoin has displayed similar volatility, falling precipitously only to rise to higher peaks. Whether this pattern will continue is not possible to predict, but the point is this:

~ Stay knowledgeable, along with your trusted advisor, about **risk-to-reward potentials of new investment concepts. Product and performance knowledge will help you determine your comfort level with speculative plays in your portfolio.**

Beware: if someone advises you to undertake a risky investment, you must ask yourself why before placing your bet.

~ **NFTs , cryptos, and precious metals are all risky.**

A trusted advisor watches and evaluates new opportunities and trends from the standpoint of your *risk tolerance* to determine what is worth adding to your portfolio.

SUMMARY

> ➤ Wise investments are for everyone, but crypto is not. Crypto is volatile but can be hugely rewarding, which is why you must seek and trust the guidance of your trusted advisor to ensure, rather than risk, your financial house and fitness.

> ➤ Cryptocurrency (while changing) is still, at this writing, defined as decentralized, and has a huge risk/reward ratio.

> ➤ Crypto in the US is (currently) classified as "property" and subject to relative taxes.

> ➤ Stay smart by staying in the know about crypto and other emerging technologies and trends. Staying informed will help you determine which opportunities are best for your portfolio.

CHAPTER TEN
Protecting Your Wealth

I'm a firm believer in the theory that people only do their best at things they truly enjoy. It is difficult to excel at something you don't enjoy.
— Jack Nicklaus

At some point, an athlete will get injured. The severity will vary, but injuries are inevitable. Athletes and their team of experts take protective measures, like stretching, ice baths, and proper technique. When an injury occurs, there are best-practices, like the RICE method: rise, ice, compress, elevate.

Injuries occur in life across the board, including financial, and most times that injury is hand in hand with physical injury.

Just as athletes take measures to prevent physical injury, we should take measures to protect our earnings and assets. We don't know when our financial houses will next get hit hard, but we know that such a time will come.

In 2009, Cristiano Ronaldo, world-famous soccer player, transferred from his English team Manchester United to the Spanish team Real Madrid for a world-record contract of $131.5 million.[149] On the opposite spectrum was a similar historic move by English soccer icon David Beckham in 2007. He agreed to a 70 percent cut in salary. Eventually, his $6.5 million annual earnings grew to over $500 million.[150]

What the two have in common is that both players took out insurance policies for their body parts—Beckham $195 million for his body and Ronaldo $144 million for his legs![151] Real Madrid players have a history of insuring their body parts. Goalkeeper Iker Casillas insured his hands for the US equivalent of $10.6 million. When he signed the deal, he joked: "If I damage my knee, I'll pretend my hand hurts."[152]

The point was to protect their livelihoods in the event they could no longer play, like most people have disability and other work-related insurance in the event of physical injury that hampers their ability to work. This precaution was especially important for Ronaldo. He consistently glided his body past players with unstoppable speed that kept his body at risk of injury.

In the 2009-2010 season, he scored an impressive 33 goals for his club in all competitions. Two seasons later, the best was yet to come. Ronaldo scored 60 goals across all competitions, and Real Madrid won La Liga with 100 points.

Highs and lows, wins and defeats are a prominent part of the economy and financial market.

Like Ronaldo and other sports greats who hold themselves to the highest standards, so should we. Ronaldo said, "I feel an endless need to learn, to improve, to evolve, not only to please the coach and the fans but also to feel satisfied with myself."[153]

He backed that up as seen by the team's and his tremendous success. Ronaldo earned 34 team honors and the Ballon d'Or award five times, awarded annually to the world's best player of the year. He understands the need for personal and family protection and wellbeing. In an interview, Ronaldo said, "The most important thing is the family. Keep your family healthy, good, and take care of your family, because this is the most important thing in the world."[154]

YOUR FINANCIAL CASTLE

Modern society's tremendous focus on asset accumulation has become far less focused on protecting those assets—and the people we love. We've become more and more a "set it and forget it" society. In contrast, think of medieval kingdoms. Formidable castles held families' tangible wealth—chests of gold and silver and walls adorned with fine tapestries and art.

What's most notable are castles' fortification measures. *Military History Now* cites fourteen fortifications. Protection for family members and their assets included tall and thick stone walls, mottes (central towers), moats (water defense), gatehouses, barbicans (protecting the gatehouses), drawbridges, and outlooks.[155]

At this writing, fortifications are in paper form as various insurance policies.

Insurance legislation was first enacted in 1601, the new means of giving property owners peace of mind. The first US mutual insurance wasn't introduced until 1735 and it wasn't until 200 years later, 1950, that the first package insurance policies were introduced for homeowners.[156] An example of how a trend can grow into a tradition, like railroads.

The two main reasons for purchasing insurance are very different: protecting and providing.

> ‣ Protecting your income and assets in case of an accident

> ‣ Providing funds for loved ones and beneficiaries after your death

Insurance bloomed into offering its own trends that have become the norm. There are so many types of insurance in the world, it's hard to know what to get, what not to get, how much, and the exact right policy for you. Since insurance is about protecting and providing for yourself and your family, a fitting illustration is to view the eight categories as mothers and the sub-categories as their offspring—in the same way we refer to corporations with subsidiaries as the "parent" company.

1. Auto—five children: (1) liability, (2) uninsured/underinsured, (3) personal injury, (4) medical payment, and (5) comprehensive and collision

2. Home—five children and a lot of variables

3. Renters—three children and several variables

4. Umbrella—no children but a lot of variables

5. Life—three children and a village of variables

6. Heath—no children but a village of variables

7. Disability—two children and several variables

8. Long-Term Care—no children but several variables

Some variables of homeowner insurance, for example, are:

- house age
- house location
- homeowner's credit history
- the insurance limits a homeowner needs

A couple of insurance offspring examples may not enter your mind, such as pet insurance, wine collection and art collection insurance, and ... body parts!

The point? Insurance, like a family tree, is complex and there's no one size fits all. Consulting with a trusted advisor will help you best determine what coverage you truly need and do not need; or you can carefully research coverages that will benefit you. Either way, the other points are to have insurance policies that

1. will protect your particular assets,

2. will protect and provide for you and your family, and

3. are tailored to your and your family's needs.

Do you know with certainty the protection and provision policies and variables you need when considering every aspect of your life?

Is there a sliver of likelihood that you're wasting your hard-earned money on policies you don't need?

For example, you're less likely to need fire insurance if you live in a rainy climate and are wise to secure if you live in a hot, dry climate.

Regarding life insurance, there's the consideration of Human Economic Life Value.

Dr. Solomon Huebner, emeritus professor of insurance at the University of Pennsylvania, developed the HLV (human life value) calculation, as defined in his book *The Economics of Life Insurance*:

> [The] value may be defined as the monetary worth of the economic forces that are incorporated within our being, namely, our character and health, our training and experience, our personality and industry, our judgment and power of initiative, and our driving force to put across in tangible form the economic images of the mind.[157]

Human economic life value considers your life in terms of what monetary worth will fully ensure your beneficiaries upon your loss of life. When you think of finances, you must consider the human economic life value. Life insurance is especially important if you have a spouse, kids, and a home.

Huebner continued:

> [Life insurance] purchase is just plain common sense from a business standpoint, and just plain decency and justice when a dependent family is involved—an ethical duty of the husband, a wife's right, and a child's claim.

> It is also important to know that the expression "life insurance protection" reaches beyond wife and children. The concept is broader in that it also extends to the insured-the premium-payer. In other words, a more balanced emphasis is required. The overwhelming majority of adults-the 98 per cent-have weaknesses along economic lines. They need to be protected through the life-insurance method against those failings as they relate to personal endeavor, health con-servation, thrift, investment, and the orderly arrangement of their monetary affairs. [158]

If you lack life insurance when you pass away, you're leaving your family in a position far more likely to struggle financially and possibly forced to move. Having insurance sufficient to pay off a home mortgage can ensure that the co-owner will keep possession of the house.

In sports, we know that eliminating the chance of injury during training and competition is impossible. But there are ways to reduce the chances. For instance, staying physically and mentally fit is crucial to lowering the likelihood of injury. An out-of-shape athlete who tries to accomplish feats that are risk high for injury are safer when physically fit.

Let's say you suffer a physical injury that prohibits you from working, and you don't have disability insurance. Your loss of income adds another injury—a financial injury.

Let's say you fall ill and have no health insurance. If you require hospitalization or extensive treatments, the financial result could be devastating to you and your family.

⤳ **Look at your lifestyle, family, and assets to determine what**

insurances are best suited for your particular needs.

Consider your smaller assets of large value. Maybe you collect high-value baseball cards or you have an extensive collection that creates high-dollar value. According to *MoneyMade*, the current value of a Topps 1952 Mickey Mantel card is $12.6 million.[159] Whoever owns that card had better have insurance.

On a lesser economic scale but higher emotional scale is that diamond ring on your spouse's finger or yours. Maybe you inherited a piece (or pieces) of valuable jewelry from your great-grandmother. The piece holds great emotional value for you and also market value.

～ Understand the risks to yourself, your family, and tangibles that can occur under your particular financial roof.

Returning to life insurance, a familiar and false narrative is that you need life insurance while you're young, to replace income for your family or business if you die prematurely, rather than later in life when you have your large, built-up net worth. In an earlier chapter, we covered the potential blind spot in that belief: facing an estate tax liability.

The Tax Cuts and Jobs Act of 2017 increased the federal estate tax exclusion amount for decedents deaths occurring from 2018 to 2025. The exclusion amount for 2022 was $12.06 million. This meant an individual could leave $12.06 million to beneficiaries and a married couple could leave $24.12 million without paying federal estate tax.[160]

In October 2022, *Forbes* posted:

> The lifetime estate and gift tax exemption (also known as the unified credit), will jump to $12.92 million in 2023, up from $12.06 million in 2022. Since couples share their exemptions, it means a wealthy couple that starts making gifts in 2023 can pass on [leave to beneficiaries] $25.84 million.[161]

This also means that an individual or married couple can gift the same amount during their lifetime and not incur a federal gift tax. The rate for the federal estate and gift tax is currently 40 percent. So, if you grow your estate, your family could end up with a significant tax due.

What if you changed the ownership in your estate from yourself to a trust outside your estate? Let's say you've grown your estate sufficient to protect and provide for your family after your death, not needing the benefit of life insurance. Ask your advisor about shifting the utility of life insurance to pay estate taxes that will be due upon your death. In that way, the need for life insurance doesn't go away but simply changed.

In addition to the cost/benefit analysis of whether an insurance purchase is smart for your circumstance, there are considerations as to whether *permanent* or *term* insurance is the better fit.

Also important is that you evaluate the insurance company(ies) you're considering.

> Does the company offer the various insurances I need?

> Is the company financially stable?

> What are the specific features of their products? For example, if you want life insurance, should you buy from a mutual insurance company or a stock insurance company?

When life insurance is the focus for estate planning, the level of complexity gets deeper.

In any case, there's enormous benefit in working with a trusted advisor, or the advisor can refer you to an insurance expert. A question for your advisor is, "Do I need life insurance or a "charitable remainder trust" (CRT)? A CRT allows you to "donate assets to charity and draw annual income for life or for a specific time period."[162] Note: The IRS is upfront in stating that they "closely examine" CRTs.[163] So if you're interested in exploring a CRT, be sure to seek and follow the advice of your trusted financial expert.

SUMMARY

› Just as an elite athlete will reduce health risks by staying in peak shape, you can reduce financial risks by keeping your financial house in peak fitness.

› Picture your financial house and all your assets as vulnerable to loss and see insurance as a castle fortifier to protect your wealth.

› Evaluate your particular needs and then select insurance policies on that basis. Insurance well-fitted for one person may not be the best for you.

› Talk with a trusted insurance expert or (better yet) your trusted advisor about your insurance needs. If you don't have either, do thorough research to educate yourself about your insurance needs and tax laws.

› Gain the insurance you need to reduce financial injury and keep more of your money!

CONCLUSION

The tragedy of life doesn't lie in not reaching your goal.
The tragedy lies in having no goal to reach.
—Benjamin E. Mayes

Make Your Finances Work for You

Well done! You've made it through this book and hopefully you're more knowledgeable about how to achieve peak financial fitness, a financial house that's well-organized, protected, and in the flow. You may have also picked up a thing or two about sporting excellence! And a bonus, tidbits from the histories of elite athletes.

The trick is to achieve the financial zone that makes your money work harder for you rather than you working hard for the money. You're the castle owner, but most people live as though the castle owns them. The more you're moving in a financial flow, the better your life will be. Your financial house in elite shape, aligned with your goals, will bring you greater joy, time, and peace of mind.

Know this:

You can achieve a lifestyle

- free from financial worry,

- money flowing and growing,

- always able to pay the bills,

- put the kids and grandkids through college,

- donate to your favorite charities,

- love life and others more,

- gain time to build deeper relationships with friends and family,

- live life your way,

- stay physically, mentally, emotionally, and financially fit,

- have fun,

- enjoy greater peace of mind,

- experience more of life, and

- leave a legacy, . . .

Those are what many people would call a successful life.

POWER FIVES

You can achieve peak financial success by

1. getting into peak fitness physically, mentally, emotionally, spiritually, and financially,

2. working hard for what you want, staying in the grind,

3. believing in yourself and the limitless possibilities,

4. seeking and using wise counsel, and

5. taking manageable steps.

Those who want an elite life will consistently

1. conquer the dragons of resistance and procrastination,

2. have a written plan,

3. embrace the grind,

4. maintain the flow zone, and

5. keep practicing.

Don't allow the power of resistance to prevent you from your best self and best life. As Steven Pressfield titled his book: *Do the Work*! Though his book doesn't specifically target financial planning, he addresses impediments to taking action, which aptly apply to pursuing optimal financial fitness.

If I had to choose only one key takeaway from *Peak Financial Fitness*, it's this:

～ Take action to optimize and fortify your financial house and every other area of your life rather than simply conceptualizing.

Of course, visualizing is the first action that creates a dream come true, but that's just the first step. Commit to memory these five power steps:

1. visualize

2. write it all down

3. shape the details into an actionable plan

4. share the plan with your trusted advisor

5. take action

In *Do the Work*, Pressfield acknowledged that going from theorizing to achieving can feel scary. But scary doesn't have to be a negative. The scare factor toward achieving your greatest dreams can be the exhilarating kind of fear: the thrill and adventure of doing the work to actualize those dreams. Know that resistance is a dragon you can slay. Consider any sport and you'll find elements of resistance. After all, overcoming and winning against resistance is the nature of athleticism. Not strictly winning over others (though that's a key point in competition), but winning over your conceived limitations by pushing yourself and pushing through the barriers.

That's winning.

That's success.

All the mistakes, step-backs, fall-downs, learning from those, and practicing through those are part of winning and success. The simple act of getting back up or learning from an error is success!

Forming a clear vision of your financial and lifestyle future and getting your financial house in alignment with your vision are some of the most rewarding experiences you can have. You're in charge, so don't allow resistance or procrastination to form regrets. There is a path of fulfillment, peace, and joy that's particular to you. And only you can stride down it and be prepared to power-zone over and around the obstacles, not allowing injuries and losses (financial, physical, emotional) to immobilize you permanently. There's a time and season for everything, which does not include *stuck*. Following a fall, we get back up—even if that takes five days or five months to work over or around.

Achieving and maintaining a fit financial house is a foundation that enables you to move through life's highs and lows with far less mental and emotional burden.

In *Charles Kuralt's America,* the famous and respected journalist eloquently described the fulfillment of doing something for the first time and the regret of not taking those steps sooner. That reminds me of the many extremely successful people I've met who sold their businesses and achieved great financial success but then settled for underachievement rather than continuing to grow.

⁓ You're either growing better or growing worse.

Which are you choosing?

Will you settle and stay stuck, or will you rise and win?

Do you know that you're innately amazing in potential? If you've been wary about that fact, another takeaway from this book is:

⁓ Take back your power!

When I think of the desire to achieve at a higher level, especially when the odds are against me, I remember Jimmy Connors' epic run as a tennis pro. His win at the 1989 Tel-Aviv Open, at the age thirty-seven (well past prime), was his 109th ATP title! But that wasn't where he stopped. He made an astounding comeback at the 1991 US Open, electrified by determination and "that insane New York energy"[164]—on his thirty-ninth birthday.

The improbability of Conners making it to the semifinals showed that age does not impede achieving success at the highest level. It's a matter of **drive and skill**.

Drive (motivation) and skill rise from the following:

1. self-will

2. making and achieving goals

3. action in practice (the grind)

4. support/advice/expertise of others

5. self-reward

Another insane comeback story is Michael Jordan's. He took some time from basketball to try pro baseball—and succeeded. He then returned to basketball and helped to lead the Chicago Bulls back to the playoffs. Note the phrase "helped to lead."

～ **Wherever you find great success, you'll find a great support team.**

In the first season of Jordan's return, his team came up short, ousted from the playoffs before the finals. Jordan wasn't deterred; he had an inner will of steel and a passion for athleticism and achieving. He practiced even harder the next year. The outcome? The Bulls won the NBA championship for the next three consecutive years.

In sports and finances are two more similarities: desire and thrill. We desire to pursue because we either need or want something, and in the grind and flow, we find the thrill of working to achieve a goal or dream. In the outcome, we find fulfillment.

I hope you'll grab hold of your *steel will* and fully engage in the grind, pursuing your dreams. I loved the grind of training for Ironman. Maybe I'll pursue that again . . . . For certain, I'll continue to pursue living life to the fullest with my fullest potential.

FINAL THOUGHT

Remember the four-legged chair and seat? In order for those five components to work powerfully as a team, they had to be assembled and secured together—nailed. Throughout *Peak Financial Fitness*, I've hammered the principles of elite performance and success. Applying the principles will enable you to achieve success at the highest levels, in whatever you want or need to pursue, including optimal financial fitness. The enormous attention paid to professional sports provided us with many examples that illustrate the principles of success. For the sake of example, I paired each of the following principles with an elite athlete or two; however, it's important to know that they all consistently practiced *all the principles*:

> ‣ **drive**—that powered Michael Jordan

> ‣ **discipline, courage, and confidence**—that powered Serena and Venus Williams

> ‣ **regimen**—that powered Tom Brady

- **knowledge-gaining**—the powered Nick Saban

- **organization**—that powered Kobe Bryant and Tom Brady

- **support experts**—that powered Jack Nicklaus

- **consistency and goal-setting**—that powered Allison Schmitt

- **zone focus**—that powered LeBron James

- **holistic approach**—that powered Derek Jeter

- **self-teaching**—that powered Bubba Watson

- **values and innovation**—that powered Dwayne Johnson

- **mentality**—that powered Danny Way

- **values**—that powered Peyton Manning

- **insurance (protection)**—that powered Christiano Ronaldo and David Beckham

- **believing**—that powered Kelsey Withrow and Jocelyn McCauley

- **grind**—that powered Michael Phelps

- **trusted advisor-coach?** See if you can find one peak-performing individual in history and in the making who didn't have a trusted advisor-coach-trainer. (The terminology is interchangeable.)

Countless studies point to this conclusion:

> ∼ **One may be born with extraordinary talent, but their expertise was refined by those who taught them.**

A *Forbes* council member wrote an article on coaching in which he quoted and agreed with a statement by mega business exec Bob Nardelli: "I absolutely believe that people, unless coached, never reach their maximum potential."[165]

Applying the principles of elite performance will power you to achieve and maintain elite financial fitness and everything else you desire in life.

‣ **Why become financially fit?** At the foundation of everything we do in life is a financial component that affects, in some small or great way, our financial houses. When you do the work to create and maintain a financially fit house—a 10 out of 10 on the scoreboard—your money will work optimally to support, serve, and protect the life you most desire to live and the legacy you most desire to leave.

‣ **Will the work of setting up or cleaning up your financial house be challenging?** Yes, but more so if you do it alone, as with any major goal. If your home needs new or repaired plumbing and you're not a certified plumber, would you do the work alone or hire an expert? That scenario perfectly illustrates the need to select, work alongside, trust, and follow the advice of a proven trusted advisor. Just as we saw how the athletes in this book worked above and beyond average effort, average training, and average preparedness, so must anyone who wants to establish or improve their financial house, their life, and their legacy.

∼ **Elite efforts produce elite outcomes.**

‣ **Even if you've already built significant wealth, is it painful to realize that your financial house is less than a 10 out of 10?** Yes, but like any realization, embracing that knowledge and putting it to work is what gets a financial house in peak fitness. Think of the stakes involved and you'll see the freedom, joy, and peace of mind you have to look forward to. You'll find that every bit of time in the grind will have been worth the effort, especially when challenging events hit your true 10 out of 10 financial house.

You can protect what you've earned and make the most of your personal resources and assets by creating or refining a financial house to work optimally for you and your family—just like an athlete in peak fitness can come through as the winner.

∼ **Become the best financial athlete you can be. You can do it!**

I leave you with one of my favorite quotes to ponder:

∼ **There is nothing noble in being superior to some other man. The true nobility is in being superior to your previous self.**[166]
—**W.L. Shelton**

Dear Reader,

With sincere gratitude, I thank you for reading *Peak Financial Fitness*. I truly hope this book has been a blessing to you in some way.

If you enjoyed this book and ordered on Amazon, please consider kindly leaving a review. Also, if you're happy enough with the book to give it a 5-star review, please share the review link on your social media, email, and by any other means. In return, I'd like to thank you by sending you a complimentary copy of my monthly newsletter with inspiring and motivational messages to move you more into flow and achieve your goals. Just send a link of your posting to: Darren@TheFinancialFlow.com

Please join my podcast, "Finding Financial Flow," by Darren Wright on Apple, Spotify, YouTube, and other social media platforms, or go to **thefinancialflow.com** for free content designed to inform and inspire you.

Gratefully,

Darren Wright, Author

NOTES

1. Peter F. Drucker, *Peter F. Drucker on Globalization.* (Boston, MA: Harvard Business Press, 2020).

2. James R. Sherman, *Rejection,* 45, (Golden Valley, MN: Pathway Books, 1982).

3. Robert O'Brien, *Marriott: The J. Willard Marriott Story,* 11, (Salt Lake City: Deseret Book Co., 1995).

4. Justin Ray, "Know Your Jack Nicklaus Numbers," PGA TOUR, May 30, 2022, https://www.pgatour.com/article/news/stats-report/2022/05/30/jack-nicklaus-numbers-the-memorial-tournament-muirfield-village-the-golden-bear.

5. Roberta Naas, "Jack Nicklaus on the Important Things in Life," Elite Traveler, January 15, 2018, https://elitetraveler.com/features/jack-nicklaus-important-things-life.

6. Ibid.

7. *YouTube,* 2018, https://youtu.be/hnHki6AW0qY.

8. Expert Panel*, "Council Post: 15 Effective Ways to Discover and Articulate Your Core Values," Forbes (Forbes Magazine, February 21, 2022), https://www.forbes.com/sites/forbescoachescouncil/2022/02/18/15-effective-ways-to-discover-and-articulate-your-core-values/?sh=5de9fd941df1.

9. "Flow State: Definition, Examples, and How to Achieve It," Medical News Today (MediLexicon International), accessed May 3, 2023, https://www.medicalnewstoday.com/articles/flow-state#.

10. IMDb, "Mario Andretti," IMDb (IMDb.com), accessed May 4, 2023, https://www.imdb.com/name/nm0004707/bio/.

11. THE WISDOM OF MARCUS AURELIUS: Selected Thoughts and Quotes for a Fulfilled Life. N.p.: Murat Durmus, 2023.

12. ScottCohnTV, "The Stories of Madoff's Victims Vary Widely, as the Fraud Continues to Unwind 10 Years Later," CNBC (CNBC, December 11, 2018), https://www.cnbc.com/2018/12/10/the-stories-of-madoffs-victims-vary-widely-a-look-10-years-out.html.

13. "Bernie Madoff," Corporate Finance Institute, March 16, 2023, https://corporatefinanceinstitute.com/resources/capital-markets/bernie-madoff/.

14. Liz Moyer, "How Regulators Missed Madoff," Forbes (Forbes Magazine, July 11, 2012), https://www.forbes.com/2009/01/27/bernard-madoff-sec-business-wall-street_0127_regulators.html?sh=fafe0a75c28d.

15. "Attorneys for Plaintiff DL IUDGE Stamton Securities and Exchange ...," accessed May 3, 2023, https://www.sec.gov/litigation/complaints/2008/comp-madoff121108.pdf.

16. Jordan Mendoza, "Who Are Some of the Celebrities Scammed in Bernie Madoff's Ponzi Scheme?," USA Today (Gannett Satellite Information Network, April 14, 2021), https://www.usatoday.com/story/money/2021/04/14/bernie-madoff-ponzi-scheme-victims-list-includes-celebrities/7223467002/.

17. _DanMangan, "Ponzi Schemer Madoff Earned $710 for Almost 3,000 Hours of Prison Work, Got 'Not Very Dependable' Review," CNBC (CNBC, July 24, 2021), https://www.cnbc.com/2021/07/23/bernie-madoff-earned-710-in-prison-after-ponzi-fraud-conviction.html.

18. Ryan Browne, "Cryptocurrency Exchange FTX Hits $32 Billion Valuation despite Bear Market Fears," CNBC (CNBC, February 1, 2022), https://www.cnbc.com/2022/01/31/crypto-exchange-ftx-valued-at-32-billion-amid-bitcoin-price-plunge.html.

19. Thomas Barrabi, "Sam Bankman-Fried Claims He 'Misaccounted' $8B in FTX Funds," New York Post (New York Post, December 23, 2022), https://nypost.com/2022/12/02/sam-bankman-fried-claims-he-misaccounted-8-billion-in-ftx-funds/.

20. Ariel Sabar, "The Billion-Dollar Ponzi Scheme That Hooked Warren Buffett and the U.S. Treasury," The Atlantic, May 9, 2023, https://www.theatlantic.com/magazine/archive/2023/06/dc-solar-power-ponzi-scheme-scandal/673782/.

21. Ibid.

22. "DC Solar Owner Sentenced to 30 Years in Prison for Billion Dollar Ponzi Scheme," Eastern District of California | DC Solar Owner Sentenced to 30 Years in Prison for Billion Dollar Ponzi Scheme | United States Department of Justice, April 19, 2023, https://www.justice.gov/usao-edca/pr/dc-solar-owner-sentenced-30-years-prison-billion-dollar-ponzi-scheme.

23. "Their House Survived Ike, but It's the Only One Left," CNN (Cable News Network), accessed May 2, 2023, https://www.cnn.com/2008/US/09/18/ike.last.house.standing/.

24. "60% Of Americans Now Living Paycheck to Paycheck, down from 64% a Month Ago," Corporate Profile, accessed May 4, 2023, https://ir.lendingclub.com/news/news-details/2023/60-of-Americans-Now-Living-Paycheck-to-Paycheck-Down-from-64-a-Month-Ago/default.aspx.

25. "Get to Know Bubba Watson," Bubba, accessed May 4, 2023, https://www.bubbawatson.com/bubba.

26. "Player Profile," OWGR, accessed May 4, 2023, https://www.owgr.com/playerprofile/bubba-watson-7334.

27. 0179wpczar, "Edmund Burke: Make Wealth Your Slave, or It Will Enslave You!," Cru Foundation, April 6, 2018, https://www.crufoundation.org/edmund-burke-make-wealth-your-slave-or-it-will-enslave-you.

28. Wayne Staats | NCAA.com, "College Football Coaches with the Most National Championships," NCAA.com (NCAA.com, January 3, 2023), https://www.ncaa.com/news/football/article/2021-01-12/college-football-coaches-most-national-championships.

29. Jim Caple, "Back in Compton, 'They Love Their Venus and Serena'," ESPN (ESPN Internet Ventures), accessed May 4, 2023, https://www.espn.com/espnw/news-commentary/story/_/id/13524355/back-compton-love-their-venus-serena.

30. Katherine Acquavella Aug 13, "Serena Williams vs. Venus Williams: A Look Back at the Williams Sisters' Historic Rivalry," CBSSports.com, August 13, 2020, https://www.cbssports.com/tennis/news/serena-williams-vs-venus-williams-a-look-back-at-the-williams-sisters-historic-rivalry/.

31. "Rick Macci Dishes on the Williams Family Stories 'King Richard' Left Out," Esquire, October 12, 2022, https://www.esquire.com/entertainment/movies/a38311899/rick-macci-king-richard-interview-true-story/.

32. Ibid.

33. Ibid.

34. "ESPN," ESPN.co.uk, accessed May 4, 2023, http://en.espn.co.uk/golf/sport/site/golflive.html.

35. "Interview with Venus Williams," CNN (Cable News Network), accessed May 4, 2023, https://www.cnn.com/2008/WORLD/asiapcf/01/23/talkasia.venus/index.html.

36. Kyle Kowalski and About Kyle Kowalski? Hi, "'Meditations' by Marcus Aurelius (Deep Book Summary + 25 Themes)," Sloww, October 29, 2021, https://www.sloww.co/meditations-marcus-aurelius/.

37. P. T. Barnum, *The Art of Money Getting: Golden Rules for Making Money* (Auckland, N.Z.: Floating Press, 2008).

38. "Michael Jordan Quote #5," 247Sports, accessed March 26, 2023, https://247sports.com/Player/80179/Quotes/Some-people-want-it-to-happen-some-wish-it-would-happen-others-m-35993908/.

39. No Author, "The Lost Decade of the Middle Class," Pew Research Center's Social & Demographic Trends Project (Pew Research Center, May 30, 2020), https://www.pewresearch.org/social-trends/2012/08/22/the-lost-decade-of-the-middle-class/.

40. "'Zen Master' NBA Coach Phil Jackson Reveals His Secrets to Success," LAist - NPR News for Southern California - 89.3 FM, July 6, 2016, https://www.kpcc.org/show/airtalk/2014-01-01/zen-master-nba-coach-phil-jackson-reveals-his-secrets-to-success.

41. A Coach's Diary, "MJ Mondays: No One Is Bigger than the Team," A Coach's Diary, accessed March 24, 2023, https://acoachsdiary.blogspot.com/2021/07/mj-mondays-no-one-is-bigger-than-team.html?m=1.

42. Lisa Capretto, "Watch: The Unorthodox Way Phil Jackson Created Champion Basketball Teams," HuffPost (HuffPost, July 17, 2013), https://www.huffpost.com/entry/phil-jackson-meditation-coaching-tactics_n_3606632.

43. Ibid.

44. "How NBA Coach Phil Jackson Taught His Teams Mindfulness | Supersoul Sunday | Oprah Winfrey Network," YouTube (YouTube, June 16, 2013), https://www.youtube.com/watch?v=aqz7R-QalqY.

45. "7 Legendary Leadership Lessons from Phil Jackson's Coaching Career," Catalyst Leader, accessed March 22, 2023, https://insider.catalystleader.com/read/7-legendary-leadership-lessons-from-phil-jacksons-coaching-career.

46. Phil Jackson and Hugh Delehanty, *Eleven Rings: The Soul of Success* (New York: Penguin Press, 2014).

47. Matt Cooper, "'Exceptionally Awesome' – the Best of Phil Mickelson's Post-PGA Championship Victory Quotes," PlanetSport (PlanetSport, May 24, 2021), https://www.planetsport.com/golf/features/phil-mickelson-quotes-wins-pga-championship.

48. Organization and ImageObject, "Tom Brady Post-Game Press Conference," Tom Brady Post-Game Press Conference, February 28, 2023, https://www.patriots.com/news/tom-brady-post-game-press-conference-119436.

49. Ajahn Brahm, *Happiness through Meditation* (Somerville, MA: Wisdom Publications, 2006).

50. "Holistic," HOLISTIC | definition in the Cambridge English Dictionary, accessed March 23, 2023, https://dictionary.cambridge.org/us/dictionary/english/holistic.

51. "Liver: Anatomy and Functions," Liver: Anatomy and Functions | Johns Hopkins Medicine, November 19, 2019, https://www.hopkinsmedicine.org/health/conditions-and-diseases/liver-anatomy-and-functions.

52. Tennis.com, "Sloane Stephens Reveals the Data and Insights That Take Her Game to the next Level," Tennis.com (Tennis.com, August 31, 2022), https://www.tennis.com/baseline/articles/sloane-stephens-qa-whoop-fitness-self-care-periods-

balance-charity-work.

53. Benjamin E. Mays and Freddie C. Colston, *Dr. Benjamin E. Mays Speaks: Representative Speeches of a Great American Orator* (Lanham, MD: University Press of America, 2002).

54. Emily Willingham, "Humans Could Live up to 150 Years, New Research Suggests," Scientific American (Scientific American, May 25, 2021), https://www.scientificamerican.com/article/humans-could-live-up-to-150-years-new-research-suggests/.

55. Ray Dalio, *Principles* (New York: Simon & Schuster, 2017)

56. "Investor Publications," SEC Emblem, May 29, 2018, https://www.sec.gov/about/reports-publications/investor-publications/introduction-529-plans.

57. Dave Ramsey and Sharon Ramsey, *Financial Peace Revisited* (New York: Viking, 2003).

58. George Shinn, *The Miracle of Motivation: The Action Guide to Happiness And Success* (Wheaton, IL: Tyndale House Publishers, 1994).

59. Zig Ziglar and Omar Akram, *Inspiration: 365 Days a Year* (Naperville, IL: Simple Truths, 2008).

60. Xtreme Spots, "Danny Way Breaks His Own Highest Air Record - Extreme Sports News," XTREMESPOTS.COM, November 24, 2018, https://www.xtremespots.com/news/danny-way-breaks-his-own-highest-air-record/.

61. "Danny Way Jumps over That Big Wall in China 2005," YouTube (YouTube, October 6, 2020), https://www.youtube.com/watch?v=HK6SG9mEtYE.

62. Steven Kotler, *The Rise of Superman: Decoding the Science of Ultimate Human Performance* (Boston: New Harvest, Houghton Mifflin Harcourt, 2014).

63. Mihaly Csikszentmihalyi, *Flow: The Psychology of Optimal Experience* (New York: Harper and Row, 2009).

64. Ibid.

65. Ibid.

66. Jack Nicklaus and Ken Bowden, *Golf My Way: The Instructional Classic, Revised and Updated* (New York: Simon & Schuster, 2005).

67. Kieron Monks, "Training the Brain to Push the Body beyond Its Limits," CNN (Cable News Network, October 20, 2015), https://www.cnn.com/2015/10/20/sport/brain-training-push-performance/index.html.

68. Karl Morris, "Neuro Putting – Why a Cool Brain Is so Important ," Irish Golfer, February 1, 2023, https://irishgolfer.ie/latest-golf-news/2023/02/02/neuro-putting-why-a-cool-brain-is-so-important/.

69. Gregory R. Samanez-Larkin, "Financial Decision Making and the Aging Brain," Association for Psychological Science - APS, April 30, 2013, https://www.psychologicalscience.org/observer/financial-decision-making-and-the-aging-brain.

70. McGonigal, Kelly. "Your Brain on Meditation," Mindful, January 26, 2022. https://www.mindful.org/your-brain-on-meditation/.

71. Steven Pressfield, *Do the Work!: Overcome Resistance and Get out of Your Own Way*, 15 (Black Irish, 2015).

72. Ibid, 64.

73. Ibid.

74. Ibid, 73.

75. Ibid, 18.

76. Ibid, 22.

77. Alex Nabaum, "When Investors Do the Most Harm with Market Timing," The Wall Street Journal, May 5, 2023, https://www.wsj.com/articles/investing-market-timing-ad3c230a.

78. Joel Beall, "Masters 2018: Sergio Garcia Sets Record with Octuple-Bogey 13 on Augusta National's 15th Hole," Golf Digest, April 5, 2018, https://www.golfdigest.com/story/masters-2018-sergio-garcia-sets-record-with-octuple-bogey-13-on-augusta-nationals-15th-hole.

79. BA Mike Oppland, "8 Traits of Flow According to Mihaly Csikszentmihalyi," PositivePsychology.com, March 9, 2023, https://positivepsychology.com/mihaly-csikszentmihalyi-father-of-flow/.

80. "Muscle Memory Definition & Meaning," Merriam-Webster (Merriam-Webster), accessed April 1, 2023, https://www.merriam-webster.com/dictionary/muscle%20memory.

81. Quotes of Michelangelo, accessed March 27, 2023, https://www.michelangelo.org/michelangelo-quotes.jsp.

82. "Precondition Definition & Meaning," Merriam-Webster, accessed May 8, 2023, https://www.merriam-webster.com/dictionary/precondition#.

83. "Get Along," Kenny Chesney - Get Along Lyrics | Lyrics.com, accessed March 30, 2023, https://www.lyrics.com/lyric/35187215/Kenny+Chesney/Get+Along.

84. "After Achieving a Dream, What Happens? 6 pro Athletes Tell," Polar Journal, March 1, 2021, https://www.polar.com/blog/6-pro-athletes-after-achieving-dream/.

85. Ibid.

86. Mario tennisracketballMario MusaMarioRacketBallI am Mario et al., "How Many People Play Tennis in the World?: 2023 Report," Tennis Racket Ball, January 18, 2023, https://tennisracketball.com/guide/how-many-people-play-tennis.

87. Sebastian Dahlman, "'1.3 Billion People Watch It, yet We Can't Have More than 400 People Living from This Sport' - Djokovic Slams System," tennis, March 2, 2023, https://tennis-infinity.com/atp/13-billion-people-watch-it-yet-we-cant-have-more-than-400-people-living-from-this-sport-djokovic-slams-system.

88. D'Arcy Maine, "'Why Am I Here, Playing for Literally $6?': The Stunning Financial Reality of pro Tennis," ESPN, accessed May 9, 2023, https://www.espn.com/tennis/story/_/id/35414286/the-stunning-financial-reality-high-cost-pro-tennis.

89. James Clear, "Continuous Improvement: How It Works and How to Master It," *James Clear*, accessed April 2, 2023, jamesclear.com/continuous-improvement.

90. *The Notebooks of Leonardo Da Vinci* (New York: Dover Publ., 1970).

91. Tim Grover, *Relentless: From Good to Great to Unstoppable*, n.d.

92. "10 Surprising Facts about Babe Ruth," History.com, accessed May 9, 2023, https://www.history.com/news/10-things-you-may-not-know-about-babe-ruth.

93. Anne, "5 Famous Athletes Who Were Told to Quit and Didn't," Discover GR8NESS, January 17, 2020, https://www.gr8ness.com/famous-athletes-who-were-told-to-quit/.

94. Ibid.

95. Ibid.

96. Ibid.

97. Musicmattersmedia, "MMM Top Ten: 10 Rejected Musicians Who Became Successful," Music Matters Media, December 12, 2022, https://musicmattersmedia.com/2022/11/30/mmm-top-10-10-rejected-musicians-who-became-successful/.

98. Barry Marshall and Barry Marshall (24 Articles Published) Tyneside, "10 Major Artists Who Were Rejected by Record Labels," TheRichest, July 12, 2015, https://www.therichest.com/expensive-lifestyle/10-major-artists-who-were-rejected-by-record-labels/.

99. Andy Nesbitt, "We Asked 9 Patriots Players to Give Their Best Tom Brady Stories and They Didn't Disappoint," USA Today (Gannett Satellite Information Network, February 1, 2023), https://ftw.usatoday.com/2023/02/tom-brady-best-stories-from-teammates.

100. "An inside Look at Tom Brady's Daily Routine," TB12, accessed April 17, 2023, https://tb12sports.com/blogs/tb12/tom-brady-daily-routine.

101. Gavin Newsham, "Everything We Know about Tom Brady's Extreme Diet and Fitness Routines," New York Post (New York Post, February 7, 2021), https://nypost.com/article/tom-brady-diet-fitness-routines/.

102. JadeScipioni, "A 9 P.m. Bedtime and Special Pajamas: Inside Tom Brady's Sleep Routine," CNBC (CNBC, February 8, 2021), https://www.cnbc.com/2021/02/06/-inside-tom-bradys-sleep-routine.html#.

103. John Breech May 11, "Tom Brady Explains What a Day in the Life of Tom Brady Is Like," CBSSports.com, May 11, 2016, https://www.cbssports.com/nfl/news/tom-brady-explains-what-a-day-in-the-life-of-tom-brady-is-like/.

104. Jeff Riedel Warren St. John, "Alabama's Nick Saban: The Scariest Man in College Football," GQ, August 26, 2013, https://www.gq.com/story/coach-nick-saban-alabama-maniac.

105. Ibid.

106. Ibid.

107. "Monte Carlo Simulation," Monte Carlo Simulation - an overview | ScienceDirect Topics, accessed April 21, 2023, https://www.sciencedirect.com/topics/economics-econometrics-and-finance/monte-carlo-simulation.

108. Maureen Farrell, "Slipping Past the Estate Tax," Forbes, July 13, 2012, https://www.forbes.com/2006/12/04/estate-tax-estee-lauder-irs-ent-law-cx_mf_1204estatetax.html?sh=2b895655c4b9.

109. "Retirement Topics - Required Minimum Distributions (Rmds)," Internal Revenue Service, accessed April 21, 2023, https://www.irs.gov/retirement-plans/plan-participant-employee/retirement-topics-required-minimum-distributions-rmds.

110. Ibid.

111. ESPN (ESPN Internet Ventures), accessed April 20, 2023, https://www.espn.com/nfl/columns/garber_greg/220770.html.

112. Seraine Page, "Navy SEAL Training Program: What It Takes to Be a Navy SEAL," Sandboxx, August 31, 2022, https://www.

sandboxx.us/blog/navy-seal-training-program-what-it-takes-to-be-a-navy-seal/.

113. Kathy Gurchiek, "Make Mental Health a Priority, Olympian Michael Phelps Urges," SHRM (SHRM, September 11, 2021), https://www.shrm.org/hr-today/news/hr-news/pages/shrm21-annual-conference-michael-phelps-mental-health.aspx.

114. "Michael Phelps' 2008 Olympics," NBC Sports, September 5, 2015, https://www.nbcsports.com/michael-phelps-2008-olympics.

115. Karen Crouse, "Michael Phelps Is Not Going to the Olympics, but His Wake Is," The New York Times (The New York Times, June 15, 2021), https://www.nytimes.com/2021/06/15/sports/olympics/michael-phelps-swimming-trials.html.

116. "Michael Phelps' Daily Routine - inside a Day in His Life," Finty, accessed April 20, 2023, https://finty.com/us/daily-routines/michael-phelps/.

117. Michael Phelps and Alan Abrahamson, No Limits: The Will to Succeed, 14, (New York: Free Press, 2008).

118. Chris Evert and Neil Amdur, Chrissie, My Own Story (New York: Simon and Schuster, 1982).

119. "Ronaldo Talent without Hard Work Is Nothing 💯 😊," YouTube, February 1, 2022, https://www.youtube.com/watch?v=fFcHEeusxL0.

120. Christine Byrne and Kelley Holland et al., "How Financial Stress Affects Your Health," EverydayHealth.com, accessed April 22, 2023, https://www.everydayhealth.com/wellness/united-states-of-stress/financial-stress-wellness-understanding-problem/.

121. Karen Harris, "A Few Favorite Quotes from Our Motivational Keynote Speakers," Asset-1@2x (cmi speaker management, November 20, 2019), https://www.cmispeakers.com/blog/a-few-favorite-quotes-from-our-motivational-keynote-speakers.

122. "Setback Definition & Meaning," Merriam-Webster (Merriam-Webster), accessed April 22, 2023, https://www.merriam-webster.com/dictionary/setback.

123. "Defeat Definition & Meaning," Merriam-Webster (Merriam-Webster), accessed April 22, 2023, https://www.merriam-webster.com/dictionary/defeat.

124. "How Michael Jordan's Mindset Made Him a Great Competitor," USA Basketball, accessed April 22, 2023, https://www.usab.com/youth/news/2012/08/how-michael-jordans-mindset-made-him-great.aspx.

125. Peter Reuell, "For Life Expectancy, Money Matters," Harvard Gazette (Harvard Gazette, March 15, 2019), https://news.harvard.edu/gazette/story/2016/04/for-life-expectancy-money-matters/.

126. ESPN, accessed May 13, 2023, http://www.espn.com/classic/biography/s/Finley_Charles.html#.

127. Charlie Finley - Sports illustrated vault | si.com, accessed May 13, 2023, https://vault.si.com/vault/1992/08/10/charlie-finley-the-former-owner-of-the-oakland-as-knows-whats-wrong-with-baseball-and-hes-more-than-happy-to-tell-you-about-it.

128. Donald Marquez, "The Charlie Finley Story, Part I (or 'The Movie That Should Have Been')," Athletics Nation, November 18, 2010, https://www.athleticsnation.com/2010/11/18/1821764/the-charlie-finley-story-part-i-or-the-movie-that-should-have-been.

129. Charlie Finley and Bugs Bunny in K.C. - Sports Illustrated Vault, accessed May 14, 2023, https://vault.si.com/vault/1961/06/05/charlie-finley-and-bugs-bunny-in-kc.

130. ESPN, accessed May 13, 2023, http://www.espn.com/classic/biography/s/Finley_Charles.html#.

131. Nick Gallo, "Why Do Stock Traders Lose Money?," FinMasters, August 31, 2022, https://finmasters.com/why-traders-lose-money/#gref.

132. Steven Pantaleo, WWE World of the Rock (DK Children, 2018).

133. Ibid.

134. "The History of Bitcoin, the First Cryptocurrency - U.S. News," accessed April 24, 2023, https://money.usnews.com/investing/articles/the-history-of-bitcoin.

135. "Full Transcript: Berkshire Hathaway Chairman & CEO Warren Buffett Speaks with CNBC's Becky Quick on 'Squawk Box' Today," CNBC (CNBC, April 12, 2023), https://www.cnbc.com/2023/04/12/full-transcript-berkshire-hathaway-chairman-ceo-warren-buffett-speaks-with-cnbcs-becky-quick-on-squawk-box-today-.html.

136. Firstadopter, "Warren Buffett Says Bitcoin Is 'Probably Rat Poison Squared'," CNBC (CNBC, May 6, 2018), https://www.cnbc.com/2018/05/05/warren-buffett-says-bitcoin-is-probably-rat-poison-squared.html.

137. Emma Newbery, "Here Are 4 of Bitcoin's Biggest Critics," The Motley Fool (The Ascent by The Motley Fool, July 17, 2021), https://www.fool.com/the-ascent/cryptocurrency/articles/here-are-4-of-bitcoins-biggest-critics/.

138. Jonathan Warner, "Former Seattle Seahawk Russell Okung Puts Half of Salary in Bitcoin, Considered Highest Paid in the League Now," RSN, February 22, 2021, https://www.nbcsports.com/northwest/seahawks/former-seattle-seahawk-russell-okung-puts-half-salary-bitcoin-considered-highest.

139. Ibid.

140. Zack Voell, "Total Cryptocurrency Market Value Hits Record $1 Trillion," CoinDesk Latest Headlines RSS (CoinDesk, March 6, 2023), https://www.coindesk.com/markets/2021/01/06/total-cryptocurrency-market-value-hits-record-1-trillion/.

141. Nelson Wang, "Billionaire Investor Bill Miller Now Has 50% of His Personal Wealth in Bitcoin," CoinDesk Latest Headlines RSS (CoinDesk, January 13, 2022), https://www.coindesk.com/business/2022/01/10/billionaire-investor-bill-miller-now-has-50-of-his-personal-wealth-in-bitcoin/.

142. IMDb, "Dwayne Johnson," IMDb (IMDb.com), accessed April 24, 2023, https://www.imdb.com/name/nm0425005/bio.

143. Raynor de Best, "Bitcoin Price History Apr 2013 - Apr 23, 2023," Statista, April 24, 2023, https://www.statista.com/statistics/326707/bitcoin-price-index/.

144. "Cryptocurrency Prices, Charts and Market Capitalizations," CoinMarketCap, accessed April 24, 2023, https://coinmarketcap.com/.

145. "Ford (F) - Market Capitalization," CompaniesMarketCap.com - companies ranked by market capitalization, accessed April 24, 2023, https://companiesmarketcap.com/ford/marketcap/.

146. Benjamin Cooper, "Analysis: Treating Crypto Fraud as Consumer Scam Gains Traction," Bloomberg Law, December 1, 2022, https://news.bloomberglaw.com/bloomberg-law-analysis/analysis-treating-crypto-fraud-as-consumer-scam-gains-traction.

147. Jordan Valinsky, "Squid Game Crypto Plunges to $0 after Scammers Steal Millions of Dollars from Investors | CNN Business," CNN (Cable News Network, November 1, 2021), https://edition.cnn.com/2021/11/01/investing/squid-game-cryptocurrency-scam/index.html.

148. "Financial Panic of 1873," U.S. Department of the Treasury, February 11, 2022, https://home.treasury.gov/about/history/freedmans-bank-building/financial-panic-of-1873.

149. Rob Hughes, "Ronaldo to Join Real Madrid for Record Price," The New York Times (The New York Times, June 11, 2009), https://www.nytimes.com/2009/06/12/sports/soccer/12iht-RONALDO.html.

150. Joe Pompliano, "The Hidden Details behind David Beckham's MLS Contract That Earned Him $500 Million," The Hidden Details Behind David Beckham's MLS Contract That Earned Him $500 Million (Huddle Up, January 4, 2023), https://huddleup.substack.com/p/the-hidden-details-behind-david-beckhams.

151. Kayla Webley, "Top 10 Oddly Insured Body Parts," Time (Time Inc., September 1, 2010), https://content.time.com/time/specials/packages/article/0,28804,2015171_2015172_2015176,00.html.

152. "Iker Casillas: The Man with the $10-Million Hands | CBC Sports," CBCnews (CBC/Radio Canada, June 4, 2010), https://www.cbc.ca/sports/soccer/iker-casillas-the-man-with-the-10-million-hands-1.895346.

153. Polina Pompliano, "The Profile Dossier: Cristiano Ronaldo, the Footballer Who Uses Hate as Fuel," Dossier: Cristiano Ronaldo, the Footballer Who Uses Hate as Fuel (The Profile, September 21, 2022), https://theprofile.substack.com/p/cristiano-ronaldo.

154. "Positive Wealth on TikTok," TikTok, accessed April 28, 2023, https://www.tiktok.com/@positivewealth101/video/7181906120670301482./

155. MilitaryHistoryNow.com, "Impregnable – 14 Brilliant Defensive Features of Medieval Castles," MilitaryHistoryNow.com, April 18, 2018, https://militaryhistorynow.com/2018/04/17/impregnable-14-brilliant-defensive-features-of-medieval-castles/.

156. "Brief History," III, May 1, 2014, https://www.iii.org/publications/insurance-handbook/brief-history#.

157. Solomon Stephen Huebner, The Economics of Life Insurance , 120, (University of Michigan, Michigan: D. Appleton, 1927).

158. Ibid.

159. "The Best Baseball Cards to Buy in 2023," MoneyMade, April 20, 2023, https://moneymade.io/learn/article/best-baseball-cards.

160. "Federal Estate Taxes," USDA ERS - Federal Estate Taxes, accessed April 28, 2023, https://www.ers.usda.gov/topics/farm-economy/federal-tax-issues/federal-estate-taxes/.

161. Janet Novack, "Lifetime Estate and Gift Tax Exemption Will Hit $12.92 Million in 2023," Forbes (Forbes Magazine, October 19, 2022), https://www.forbes.com/sites/janetnovack/2022/10/18/new-higher-estate-and-gift-tax-limits-for-2023-couples-can-pass-on-extra-172-million-tax-free/?sh=1a7980147dd8.

162. "Charitable Remainder Trusts," Internal Revenue Service, accessed April 28, 2023, https://www.irs.gov/charities-non-profits/charitable-remainder-trusts.

163. Ibid.

164. Tennis.com, "1991: Jimmy Connors' Gripping U.S. Open Run at Age 39," Tennis.com, September 10, 2015, https://www.tennis.com/news/articles/1991-jimmy-connors-gripping-u-s-open-run-at-age-39.

165. Keir Weimer, "Council Post: You've Decided to Work with a Coach -- Now What?," Forbes (Forbes Magazine, March 16, 2020), https://www.forbes.com/sites/forbesbusinesscouncil/2020/03/16/youve-decided-to-work-with-a-coach-now-what/?sh=545ace7965af.

166. "Ethical Addresses and Ethical Record," Google Books (Google), accessed April 30, 2023, https://www.google.com/books/edition/Ethical_Addresses_and_Ethical_Record/9oFQAQAAMAAJ?hl=en&gbpv=1.

BIBLIOGRAPHY

0179wpczar. "Edmund Burke: Make Wealth Your Slave, or It Will Enslave You!" Cru Foundation, April 6, 2018. https://www.crufoundation.org/edmund-burke-make-wealth-your-slave-or-it-will-enslave-you.

"10 Surprising Facts about Babe Ruth." History.com. Accessed May 9, 2023. https://www.history.com/news/10-things-you-may-not-know-about-babe-ruth.

"60% Of Americans Now Living Paycheck to Paycheck, down from 64% a Month Ago." Corporate Profile. Accessed May 4, 2023. https://ir.lendingclub.com/news/news-details/2023/60-of-Americans-Now-Living-Paycheck-to-Paycheck-Down-from-64-a-Month-Ago/default.aspx.

"7 Legendary Leadership Lessons from Phil Jackson's Coaching Career." Catalyst Leader. Accessed March 22, 2023. https://insider.catalystleader.com/read/7-legendary-leadership-lessons-from-phil-jacksons-coaching-career.

"After Achieving a Dream, What Happens? 6 pro Athletes Tell." Polar Journal, March 1, 2021. https://www.polar.com/blog/6-pro-athletes-after-achieving-dream/.

"An inside Look at Tom Brady's Daily Routine." TB12. Accessed April 17, 2023. https://tb12sports.com/blogs/tb12/tom-brady-daily-routine.

Anne. "5 Famous Athletes Who Were Told to Quit and Didn't." Discover GR8NESS, January 17, 2020. https://www.gr8ness.com/famous-athletes-who-were-told-to-quit/.

"Attorneys for Plaintiff DL IUDGE Stamton Securities and Exchange ..." Accessed May 3, 2023. https://www.sec.gov/litigation/complaints/2008/comp-madoff121108.pdf.

Author, No. "The Lost Decade of the Middle Class." Pew Research Center's Social & Demographic Trends Project. Pew Research Center, May 30, 2020. https://www.pewresearch.org/social-trends/2012/08/22/the-lost-decade-of-the-middle-class/.

Beall, Joel. "Masters 2018: Sergio Garcia Sets Record with Octuple-Bogey 13 on Augusta National's 15th Hole." Golf Digest, April 5, 2018. https://www.golfdigest.com/story/masters-2018-sergio-garcia-sets-record-with-octuple-bogey-13-on-augusta-15th-hole.

Barnum, P. T. *The Art of Money Getting: Golden Rules for Making Money*. Auckland, N.Z.: Floating Press, 2008.

Barrabi, Thomas. "Sam Bankman-Fried Claims He 'Misaccounted' $8B in FTX Funds." New York Post. New York Post, December 23, 2022. https://nypost.com/2022/12/02/sam-bankman-fried-claims-he-misaccounted-8-billion-in-ftx-funds/.

"Bernie Madoff." Corporate Finance Institute, March 16, 2023. https://corporatefinanceinstitute.com/resources/capital-markets/bernie-madoff/.

Best, Raynor de. "Bitcoin Price History Apr 2013 - Apr 23, 2023." Statista, April 24, 2023. https://www.statista.com/statistics/326707/bitcoin-price-index/.

Brahm, Ajahn. *Happiness through Meditation*. Somerville, MA: Wisdom Publications, 2006.

"Brief History." III, May 1, 2014. https://www.iii.org/publications/insurance-handbook/brief-history#.

Browne, Ryan. "Cryptocurrency Exchange FTX Hits $32 Billion Valuation despite Bear Market Fears." CNBC. CNBC, February 1, 2022. https://www.cnbc.com/2022/01/31/crypto-exchange-ftx-valued-at-32-billion-amid-bitcoin-price-plunge.html.

Caple, Jim. "Back in Compton, 'They Love Their Venus and Serena'." ESPN. ESPN Internet Ventures. Accessed May 4, 2023. https://www.espn.com/espnw/news-commentary/story/_/id/13524355/back-compton-love-their-venus-serena.

Capretto, Lisa. "Watch: The Unorthodox Way Phil Jackson Created Champion Basketball Teams." HuffPost. HuffPost, July 17, 2013. https://www.huffpost.com/entry/phil-jackson-meditation-coaching-tactics_n_3606632.

"Charitable Remainder Trusts." Internal Revenue Service. Accessed April 28, 2023. https://www.irs.gov/charities-non-profits/charitable-remainder-trusts.

Charlie Finley and Bugs Bunny in K.C. - Sports Illustrated Vault. Accessed May 14, 2023. https://vault.si.com/vault/1961/06/05/charlie-finley-and-bugs-bunny-in-kc.

Charlie Finley - Sports illustrated vault | si.com. Accessed May 13, 2023. https://vault.si.com/vault/1992/08/10/charlie-finley-the-former-owner-of-the-oakland-as-knows-whats-wrong-with-baseball-and-hes-more-than-happy-to-tell-you-about-it.

"Continuous Improvement: How It Works and How to Master It." James Clear, August 31, 2022. https://jamesclear.com/continuous-improvement.

Cooper, Benjamin. "Analysis: Treating Crypto Fraud as Consumer Scam Gains Traction." Bloomberg Law, December 1, 2022. https://news.bloomberglaw.com/bloomberg-law-analysis/analysis-treating-crypto-fraud-as-consumer-scam-gains-traction.

Cooper, Matt. "'Exceptionally Awesome' – the Best of Phil Mickelson's Post-PGA Championship Victory Quotes." PlanetSport. PlanetSport, May 24, 2021. https://www.planetsport.com/golf/features/phil-mickelson-quotes-wins-pga-championship.

Crouse, Karen. "Michael Phelps Is Not Going to the Olympics, but His Wake Is." The New York Times. The New York Times, June 15, 2021. https://www.nytimes.com/2021/06/15/sports/olympics/michael-phelps-swimming-trials.html.

"Cryptocurrency Prices, Charts and Market Capitalizations." CoinMarketCap. Accessed April 24, 2023. https://coinmarketcap.com/.

Csikszentmihalyi, Mihaly. *Flow: The psychology of optimal experience*. New York: Harper and Row, 2009.

Dahlman, Sebastian. "'1.3 Billion People Watch It, yet We Can't Have More than 400 People Living from This Sport' - Djokovic Slams System." tennis, March 2, 2023. https://tennis-infinity.com/atp/13-billion-people-watch-it-yet-we-cant-have-more-than-400-people-living-from-this-sport-djokovic-slams-system.

Dalio, Ray. *Principles*. New York: Simon & Schuster, 2017.

_DanMangan. "Ponzi Schemer Madoff Earned $710 for Almost 3,000 Hours of Prison Work, Got 'Not Very Dependable' Review." CNBC. CNBC, July 24, 2021. https://www.cnbc.com/2021/07/23/bernie-madoff-earned-710-in-prison-after-ponzi-fraud-conviction.html.

"Danny Way Jumps over That Big Wall in China 2005." YouTube. YouTube, October 6, 2020. https://www.youtube.com/watch?v=HK6SG9mEtYE.

"DC Solar Owner Sentenced to 30 Years in Prison for Billion Dollar Ponzi Scheme." Eastern District of California | DC Solar Owner Sentenced to 30 Years in Prison for Billion Dollar Ponzi Scheme | United States Department of Justice, April 19, 2023. https://www.justice.gov/usao-edca/pr/dc-solar-owner-sentenced-30-years-prison-billion-dollar-ponzi-scheme.

"Defeat Definition & Meaning." Merriam-Webster. Merriam-Webster. Accessed April 22, 2023. https://www.merriam-webster.com/dictionary/defeat.

"Despite 6 Years into Retirement, Michael Phelps Has Not Gone Soft on His Workout Regimen: 'Lightweight or No Weight...but It Kicked My A**.'" EssentiallySports, January 6, 2023. https://www.essentiallysports.com/us-sports-news-swimming-news-despite-6-years-into-retirement-michael-phelps-has-not-gone-soft-on-his-workout-regimen-lightweight-or-no-weight-but-it-kicked-my-a/.

Deveney, Sean. "A Medical Expert Predicted 2011 Post-Lockout Injury Spike. Now He Has a Warning for the NBA's Return." Forbes, July 1, 2020. https://www.forbes.com/sites/seandeveney/2020/06/30/he-predicted-post-lockout-injury-spike-in-2011-now-he-has-a-warning-for-the-nba/?sh=450079a22a91.

Diary, A Coach's. "MJ Mondays: No One Is Bigger than the Team." A Coach's Diary. Accessed March 24, 2023. https://acoachsdiary.blogspot.com/2021/07/mj-mondays-no-one-is-bigger-than-team.html?m=1.

Drucker, Peter F. 2020. *Peter F. Drucker on Globalization*. Boston, MA: Harvard Business Press.

"ESPN." ESPN.co.uk. Accessed May 4, 2023. http://en.espn.co.uk/golf/sport/site/golflive.html.

ESPN. ESPN Internet Ventures. Accessed April 23, 2023. https://www.espn.com/classic/s/finleyquotes000817.html.

ESPN. ESPN Internet Ventures. Accessed April 20, 2023. https://www.espn.com/nfl/columns/garber_greg/220770.html.

"Ethical Addresses and Ethical Record." Google Books. Accessed April 30, 2023. https://www.google.com/books/edition/Ethical_Addresses_and_Ethical_Record/9oFQAQAAMAAJ?hl=en&gbpv=1.

Evert, Chris, and Neil Amdur. *Chrissie, My Own Story*. New York: Simon & Schuster, 1982.

Farrell, Maureen. "Slipping Past the Estate Tax." Forbes, July 13, 2012. https://www.forbes.com/2006/12/04/estate-tax-estee-lauder-irs-ent-law-cx_mf_1204estatetax.html?sh=2b895655c4b9.

"Federal Estate Taxes." USDA ERS - Federal Estate Taxes. Accessed April 28, 2023. https://www.ers.usda.gov/topics/farm-economy/federal-tax-issues/federal-estate-taxes/.

"Financial Panic of 1873." U.S. Department of the Treasury, February 11, 2022. https://home.treasury.gov/about/history/freedmans-bank-building/financial-panic-of-1873.

Firstadopter. "Warren Buffett Says Bitcoin Is 'Probably Rat Poison Squared'." CNBC. CNBC, May 6, 2018. https://www.cnbc.com/2018/05/05/warren-buffett-says-bitcoin-is-probably-rat-poison-squared.html.

"Flow State: Definition, Examples, and How to Achieve It." Medical News Today. MediLexicon International. Accessed May 3, 2023. https://www.medicalnewstoday.com/articles/flow-state#.

"Ford (F) - Market Capitalization." CompaniesMarketCap.com - companies ranked by market capitalization. Accessed April 24, 2023. https://companiesmarketcap.com/ford/marketcap/.

"Full Transcript: Berkshire Hathaway Chairman & CEO Warren Buffett Speaks with CNBC's Becky Quick on 'Squawk Box' Today." CNBC. CNBC, April 12, 2023. https://www.cnbc.com/2023/04/12/full-transcript-berkshire-hathaway-chairman-ceo-warren-buffett-speaks-with-cnbcs-becky-quick-on-squawk-box-today-.html.

Gallo, Nick. "Why Do Stock Traders Lose Money?" FinMasters, August 31, 2022. https://finmasters.com/why-traders-lose-money/#gref.

"Get Along." Kenny Chesney - Get Along Lyrics | Lyrics.com. Accessed March 30, 2023. https://www.lyrics.com/lyric/35187215/Kenny+Chesney/Get+Along.

"Get to Know Bubba Watson." Bubba. Accessed May 4, 2023. https://www.bubbawatson.com/bubba.

Goodkind, Nicole, Julia Horowitz, and David Goldman. "Goodbye 2022 -- and Good Riddance. Markets Close out Their Worst Year since 2008 | CNN Business." CNN. Cable News Network, December 30, 2022. https://www.cnn.com/2022/12/30/investing/dow-stock-market-2022/index.html.

Grover, Tim. *Relentless: From Good to Great to Unstoppable*, n.d.

Gruver, Ed. *Hairs vs. Squares: The Mustache Gang, the Big Red Machine, and the Tumultuous Summer of '72*. Lincoln: University of Nebraska Press, 2016.

Gsass. "Navigating the Market Turmoil." BlackRock. Accessed April 10, 2023. https://www.blackrock.com/ca/investors/en/market-insights/navigating-market-turmoil?switchLocale=y&siteEntryPassthrough=true.

Gurchiek, Kathy. "Make Mental Health a Priority, Olympian Michael Phelps Urges." SHRM. SHRM, September 11, 2021. https://www.shrm.org/hr-today/news/hr-news/pages/shrm21-annual-conference-michael-phelps-mental-health.aspx.

Harris, Karen. "A Few Favorite Quotes from Our Motivational Keynote Speakers." Asset-1@2x. cmi speaker management, November 20, 2019. https://www.cmispeakers.com/blog/a-few-favorite-quotes-from-our-motivational-keynote-speakers.

Helman, Christopher. "Solar Power Ponzi Couple Pleads Guilty in Billion-Dollar Fraud." Forbes, January 27, 2020. https://

www.forbes.com/sites/christopherhelman/2020/01/27/solar-power-ponzi-couple-pleads-guilty-in-billion-dollar-fraud/?sh=1e81d2c11153.

Hill, Napoleon. *The Law of Success*. New York, NY: TarcherPerigee, an imprint of Penguin Random House LLC, 2017.

"Holistic." HOLISTIC | definition in the Cambridge English Dictionary. Accessed March 23, 2023. https://dictionary.cambridge.org/us/dictionary/english/holistic.

Holland, Christine Byrne and Kelley, Kelly Kennedy, Paula Derrow, Lorie A. Parch, Don Rauf, Karla Walsh, Everyday Health Editors, Lisa Rapaport, and Marisa Petrarca. "How Financial Stress Affects Your Health." EverydayHealth.com. Accessed April 22, 2023. https://www.everydayhealth.com/wellness/united-states-of-stress/financial-stress-wellness-understanding-problem/.

"How Michael Jordan's Mindset Made Him a Great Competitor." USA Basketball. Accessed April 22, 2023. https://www.usab.com/youth/news/2012/08/how-michael-jordans-mindset-made-him-great.aspx.

"How NBA Coach Phil Jackson Taught His Teams Mindfulness | Supersoul Sunday | Oprah Winfrey Network." YouTube. YouTube, June 16, 2013. https://www.youtube.com/watch?v=aqz7R-QalqY.

Huebner, Solomon Stephen. *The Economics of Life Insurance*. University of Michigan, Michigan: D. Appleton, 1927.

Hughes, Rob. "Ronaldo to Join Real Madrid for Record Price." The New York Times. The New York Times, June 11, 2009. https://www.nytimes.com/2009/06/12/sports/soccer/12iht-RONALDO.html.

"Human Life Value: The Forgotten Standard of Life Insurance." Monegenix®, February 2, 2023. https://www.monegenix.com/human-life-value/.

"Iker Casillas: The Man with the $10-Million Hands | CBC Sports." CBCnews. CBC/Radio Canada, June 4, 2010. https://www.cbc.ca/sports/soccer/iker-casillas-the-man-with-the-10-million-hands-1.895346.

IMDb. "Dwayne Johnson." IMDb. IMDb.com. Accessed April 24, 2023. https://www.imdb.com/name/nm0425005/bio.

IMDb. "Mario Andretti." IMDb. IMDb.com. Accessed May 4, 2023. https://www.imdb.com/name/nm0004707/bio/.

"Interview with Venus Williams." CNN. Cable News Network. Accessed May 4, 2023. https://www.cnn.com/2008/WORLD/asiapcf/01/23/talkasia.venus/index.html.

"Investor Publications." SEC Emblem, May 29, 2018. https://www.sec.gov/about/reports-publications/investor-publications/introduction-529-plans.

Jackson, Phil, and Hugh Delehanty. *Eleven Rings: The Soul of Success*. New York: Penguin Press, 2014.

JadeScipioni. "A 9 P.m. Bedtime and Special Pajamas: Inside Tom Brady's Sleep Routine." CNBC. CNBC, February 8, 2021. https://www.cnbc.com/2021/02/06/-inside-tom-bradys-sleep-routine.html.

John Breech May 11. "Tom Brady Explains What a Day in the Life of Tom Brady Is Like." CBSSports.com, May 11, 2016. https://www.cbssports.com/nfl/news/tom-brady-explains-what-a-day-in-the-life-of-tom-brady-is-like/.

Jonathan Warner. "Former Seattle Seahawk Russell Okung Puts Half of Salary in Bitcoin, Considered Highest Paid in the League Now." RSN, February 22, 2021. https://www.nbcsports.com/northwest/seahawks/former-seattle-seahawk-russell-okung-puts-half-salary-bitcoin-considered-highest.

Katherine Acquavella Aug 13. "Serena Williams vs. Venus Williams: A Look Back at the Williams Sisters' Historic Rivalry." CBSSports.com, August 13, 2020. https://www.cbssports.com/tennis/news/serena-williams-vs-venus-williams-a-look-back-at-the-williams-sisters-historic-rivalry/.

Kotler, Steven. *The Rise of Superman: Decoding the Science of Ultimate Human Performance*. Boston: New Harvest, Houghton Mifflin Harcourt, 2014.

Kowalski, Kyle, and About Kyle Kowalski? Hi. "'Meditations' by Marcus Aurelius (Deep Book Summary + 25 Themes)." Sloww, October 29, 2021. https://www.sloww.co/meditations-marcus-aurelius/.

"Lesson 10: Uses of Life Insurance." 10.1.1 Human Life Value Approach. Accessed May 15, 2023. https://course.uceusa.com/courses/content/405/page_315.htm.

Letter to Darren Wright. *Compliance - DJIA*, June 28, 2023.

"Liver: Anatomy and Functions." Liver: Anatomy and Functions | Johns Hopkins Medicine, November 19, 2019. https://www.hopkinsmedicine.org/health/conditions-and-diseases/liver-anatomy-and-functions.

Maine, D'Arcy. "'Why Am I Here, Playing for Literally $6?': The Stunning Financial Reality of pro Tennis." ESPN. ESPN Internet Ventures, January 18, 2023. https://www.espn.com/tennis/story/_/id/35414286/the-stunning-financial-reality-high-cost-pro-tennis.

Mario, Mario tennisracketballMario MusaMarioRacketBallI am, Mario tennisracketballMario MusaMarioRacketBall, Mario, Tennisracketball, Mario Musa, and MarioRacketBall. "How Many People Play Tennis in the World?: 2023 Report." Tennis Racket Ball, January 18, 2023. https://tennisracketball.com/guide/how-many-people-play-tennis.

Marquez, Donald. "The Charlie Finley Story, Part I (or 'The Movie That Should Have Been')." Athletics Nation, November 18, 2010. https://www.athleticsnation.com/2010/11/18/1821764/the-charlie-finley-story-part-i-or-the-movie-that-should-have-been.

Marshall, Barry, and Barry Marshall (24 Articles published) Tyneside. "10 Major Artists Who Were Rejected by Record Labels." TheRichest, July 12, 2015. https://www.therichest.com/expensive-lifestyle/10-major-artists-who-were-rejected-by-record-labels/.

Mays, Benjamin E., and Freddie C. Colston. *Dr. Benjamin E. Mays Speaks: Representative Speeches of a Great American Orator*. Lanham, MD: University Press of America, 2002.

McGonigal, Kelly. "Your Brain on Meditation." Mindful, January 26, 2022. https://www.mindful.org/your-brain-on-meditation/.

Mendoza, Jordan. "Who Are Some of the Celebrities Scammed in Bernie Madoff's Ponzi Scheme?" USA Today. Gannett Satellite Information Network, April 14, 2021. https://www.usatoday.com/story/money/2021/04/14/bernie-madoff-ponzi-scheme-victims-list-includes-celebrities/7223467002/.

"Michael Jordan Quote #5." 247Sports. Accessed March 26, 2023. https://247sports.com/Player/80179/Quotes/Some-people-want-it-to-happen-some-wish-it-would-happen-others-m-35993908/.

"Michael Phelps' 2008 Olympics." NBC Sports, September 5, 2015. https://www.nbcsports.com/michael-phelps-2008-olympics.

"Michael Phelps' Daily Routine - inside a Day in His Life." Finty. Accessed April 20, 2023. https://finty.com/us/daily-routines/michael-phelps/.

Mike Oppland, BA. "8 Traits of Flow According to Mihaly Csikszentmihalyi." PositivePsychology.com, March 9, 2023. https://positivepsychology.com/mihaly-csikszentmihalyi-father-of-flow/.

MilitaryHistoryNow.com. "Impregnable – 14 Brilliant Defensive Features of Medieval Castles." MilitaryHistoryNow.com, April 18, 2018. https://militaryhistorynow.com/2018/04/17/impregnable-14-brilliant-defensive-features-of-medieval-castles/.

Monks, Kieron. "Training the Brain to Push the Body beyond Its Limits." CNN. Cable News Network, October 20, 2015. https://www.cnn.com/2015/10/20/sport/brain-training-push-performance/index.html.

"Monte Carlo Simulation." Monte Carlo Simulation - an overview | ScienceDirect Topics. Accessed April 21, 2023. https://www.sciencedirect.com/topics/economics-econometrics-and-finance/monte-carlo-simulation.

Morris, Karl. "Neuro Putting – Why a Cool Brain Is so Important ." Irish Golfer, February 1, 2023. https://irishgolfer.ie/latest-golf-news/2023/02/02/neuro-putting-why-a-cool-brain-is-so-important/.

Moyer, Liz. "How Regulators Missed Madoff." Forbes. Forbes Magazine, July 11, 2012. https://www.forbes.com/2009/01/27/bernard-madoff-sec-business-wall-street_0127_regulators.html?sh=fafe0a75c28d.

"Muscle memory Definition & Meaning." Merriam-Webster. Merriam-Webster. Accessed April 1, 2023. https://www.merriam-webster.com/dictionary/muscle%20memory.

Musicmattersmedia. "MMM Top Ten: 10 Rejected Musicians Who Became Successful." Music Matters Media, December 12, 2022. https://musicmattersmedia.com/2022/11/30/mmm-top-10-10-rejected-musicians-who-became-successful/.

Naas, Roberta. "Jack Nicklaus on the Important Things in Life." Elite Traveler, January 15, 2018. https://elitetraveler.com/features/jack-nicklaus-important-things-life.

Nabaum, Alex. "When Investors Do the Most Harm with Market Timing." The Wall Street Journal, May 5, 2023. https://www.wsj.com/articles/investing-market-timing-ad3c230a.

NCAA.com, Wayne Staats |. "College Football Coaches with the Most National Championships." NCAA.com. NCAA.com, January 3, 2023. https://www.ncaa.com/news/football/article/2021-01-12/college-football-coaches-most-national-championships.

Nesbitt, Andy. "We Asked 9 Patriots Players to Give Their Best Tom Brady Stories and They Didn't Disappoint." USA Today. Gannett Satellite Information Network, February 1, 2023. https://ftw.usatoday.com/2023/02/tom-brady-best-stories-from-teammates.

Newbery, Emma. "Here Are 4 of Bitcoin's Biggest Critics." The Motley Fool. The Ascent by The Motley Fool, July 17, 2021. https://www.fool.com/the-ascent/cryptocurrency/articles/here-are-4-of-bitcoins-biggest-critics/.

Newsham, Gavin. "Everything We Know about Tom Brady's Extreme Diet and Fitness Routines." New York Post. New York Post, February 7, 2021. https://nypost.com/article/tom-brady-diet-fitness-routines/.

Nicklaus, Jack, and Ken Bowden. Golf My Way: The Instructional Classic, Revised and Updated. New York: Simon & Schuster, 2005.

Novack, Janet. "Lifetime Estate and Gift Tax Exemption Will Hit $12.92 Million in 2023." Forbes. Forbes Magazine, October 19, 2022. https://www.forbes.com/sites/janetnovack/2022/10/18/new-higher-estate-and-gift-tax-limits-for-2023-couples-can-pass-on-extra-172-million-tax-free/?sh=1a7980147dd8.

O'Brien, Robert. Marriott: The J. Willard Marriott story, 11. Salt Lake City: Deseret Book Co., 1995.

Organization, and ImageObject. "Tom Brady Post-Game Press Conference." Tom Brady Post-Game Press Conference, February 28, 2023. https://www.patriots.com/news/tom-brady-post-game-press-conference-119436.

Page, Seraine. "Navy SEAL Training Program: What It Takes to Be a Navy SEAL." Sandboxx, August 31, 2022. https://www.sandboxx.us/blog/navy-seal-training-program-what-it-takes-to-be-a-navy-seal/.

Panel®, Expert. "Council Post: 15 Effective Ways to Discover and Articulate Your Core Values." Forbes. Forbes Magazine, February 21, 2022. https://www.forbes.com/sites/forbescoachescouncil/2022/02/18/15-effective-ways-to-discover-and-articulate-your-core-values/?sh=5de9fd941df1.

Pantaleo, Steven. WWE World of the Rock. DK Children, 2018.

Phelps, Michael, and Alan Abrahamson. No Limits: The Will to Succeed. New York: Free Press, 2008.

"Player Profile." OWGR. Accessed May 4, 2023. https://www.owgr.com/playerprofile/bubba-watson-7334.

Pompliano, Joe. "The Hidden Details behind David Beckham's MLS Contract That Earned Him $500 Million." The Hidden Details Behind David Beckham's MLS Contract That Earned Him $500 Million. Huddle Up, January 4, 2023. https://huddleup.substack.com/p/the-hidden-details-behind-david-beckhams.

Pompliano, Polina. "The Profile Dossier: Cristiano Ronaldo, the Footballer Who Uses Hate as Fuel." Dossier: Cristiano Ronaldo, the Footballer Who Uses Hate as Fuel. The Profile, September 21, 2022. https://theprofile.substack.com/p/cristiano-ronaldo.

"Positive Wealth on TikTok." TikTok. Accessed April 28, 2023. https://www.tiktok.com/@positivewealth101/video/7181906120670301482.

"Precondition Definition & Meaning." Merriam-Webster. Accessed May 8, 2023. https://www.merriam-webster.com/dictionary/precondition#.

Pressfield, Steven. Do the Work!: Overcome Resistance and Get out of Your Own Way. Black Irish, 2015.

Quotes of Michelangelo. Accessed March 27, 2023. https://www.michelangelo.org/michelangelo-quotes.jsp

Ramsey, Dave, and Sharon Ramsey. *Financial Peace Revisited*. New York: Viking, 2003.

Ray, Justin. "Know Your Jack Nicklaus Numbers." PGA TOUR, May 30, 2022. https://www.pgatour.com/article/news/stats-report/2022/05/30/jack-nicklaus-numbers-the-memorial-tournament-muirfield-village-the-golden-bear.

"Retirement Topics - Required Minimum Distributions (Rmds)." Internal Revenue Service. Accessed April 21, 2023. https://www.irs.gov/retirement-plans/plan-participant-employee/retirement-topics-required-minimum-distributions-rmds.

Reuell, Peter. "For Life Expectancy, Money Matters." Harvard Gazette. Harvard Gazette, March 15, 2019. https://news.harvard.edu/gazette/story/2016/04/for-life-expectancy-money-matters/.

"Rick Macci Dishes on the Williams Family Stories 'King Richard' Left Out." Esquire, October 12, 2022. https://www.esquire.com/entertainment/movies/a38311899/rick-macci-king-richard-interview-true-story/.

"Ronaldo Talent without Hard Work Is Nothing 💯 😊." YouTube, February 1, 2022. https://www.youtube.com/watch?v=fFcHEeusxL0.

Sabar, Ariel. "The Billion-Dollar Ponzi Scheme That Hooked Warren Buffett and the U.S. Treasury." The Atlantic, May 9, 2023. https://www.theatlantic.com/magazine/archive/2023/06/dc-solar-power-ponzi-scheme-scandal/673782/.

Samanez-Larkin, Gregory R. "Financial Decision Making and the Aging Brain." Association for Psychological Science - APS, April 30, 2013. https://www.psychologicalscience.org/observer/financial-decision-making-and-the-aging-brain.

ScottCohnTV. "The Stories of Madoff's Victims Vary Widely, as the Fraud Continues to Unwind 10 Years Later." CNBC. CNBC, December 11, 2018. https://www.cnbc.com/2018/12/10/the-stories-of-madoffs-victims-vary-widely-a-look-10-years-out.html.

"Setback Definition & Meaning." Merriam-Webster. Merriam-Webster. Accessed April 22, 2023. https://www.merriam-webster.com/dictionary/setback.

Sherman, James R. *Rejection*, 45. Golden Valley, MN: Pathway Books, 1982.

Shinn, George. *The Miracle of Motivation: The Action Guide to Happiness And Success*. Wheaton, IL: Tyndale House Publishers, 1994.

Spots, Xtreme. "Danny Way Breaks His Own Highest Air Record - Extreme Sports News." XTREMESPOTS.COM, November 24, 2018. https://www.xtremespots.com/news/danny-way-breaks-his-own-highest-air-record/.

Tennis.com. "1991: Jimmy Connors' Gripping U.S. Open Run at Age 39." Tennis.com, September 10, 2015. https://www.tennis.com/news/articles/1991-jimmy-connors-gripping-u-s-open-run-at-age-39.

Tennis.com. "Sloane Stephens Reveals the Data and Insights That Take Her Game to the next Level." Tennis.com. Tennis.com, August 31, 2022. https://www.tennis.com/baseline/articles/sloane-stephens-qa-whoop-fitness-self-care-periods-balance-charity-work.

"The Best Baseball Cards to Buy in 2023." MoneyMade, April 20, 2023. https://moneymade.io/learn/article/best-baseball-cards.

"The History of Bitcoin, the First Cryptocurrency - U.S. News." Accessed April 24, 2023. https://money.usnews.com/investing/articles/the-history-of-bitcoin.

The Notebooks of Leonardo Da Vinci. New York: Dover Publ., 1970.

The Wisdom of Marcus Aurelius: Selected Thoughts and Quotes for a Fulfilled Life. N.p.: Murat Durmus, 2023.

"Their House Survived Ike, but It's the Only One Left." CNN. Cable News Network. Accessed May 2, 2023. https://www.cnn.com/2008/US/09/18/ike.last.house.standing/.

Valinsky, Jordan. "Squid Game Crypto Plunges to $0 after Scammers Steal Millions of Dollars from Investors | CNN Business." CNN. Cable News Network, November 1, 2021. https://edition.cnn.com/2021/11/01/investing/squid-game-cryptocurrency-scam/index.html.

Voell, Zack. "Total Cryptocurrency Market Value Hits Record $1 Trillion." CoinDesk Latest Headlines RSS. CoinDesk, March 6, 2023. https://www.coindesk.com/markets/2021/01/06/total-cryptocurrency-market-value-hits-record-1-trillion/.

Wang, Nelson. "Billionaire Investor Bill Miller Now Has 50% of His Personal Wealth in Bitcoin." CoinDesk Latest Headlines RSS. CoinDesk, January 13, 2022. https://www.coindesk.com/business/2022/01/10/billionaire-investor-bill-miller-now-has-50-of-his-personal-wealth-in-bitcoin/.

Warren St. John, Jeff Riedel. "Alabama's Nick Saban: The Scariest Man in College Football." GQ, August 26, 2013. https://www.gq.com/story/coach-nick-saban-alabama-maniac.

Webley, Kayla. "Top 10 Oddly Insured Body Parts." Time. Time Inc., September 1, 2010. https://content.time.com/time/specials/packages/article/0,28804,2015171_2015172_2015176,00.html.

Weimer, Keir. "Council Post: You've Decided to Work with a Coach -- Now What?" Forbes, March 16, 2020. https://www.forbes.com/sites/forbesbusinesscouncil/2020/03/16/youve-decided-to-work-with-a-coach-now-what/?sh=545ace7965af.

Willingham, Emily. "Humans Could Live up to 150 Years, New Research Suggests." Scientific American. Scientific American, May 25, 2021. https://www.scientificamerican.com/article/humans-could-live-up-to-150-years-new-research-suggests/.

Writer, Times Staff. "Kobe's Nike Ad to Debut." Tampa Bay Times. Tampa Bay Times, December 10, 2019. https://www.tampabay.com/archive/2006/02/09/kobe-s-nike-ad-to-debut/.

YouTube, 2018. https://youtu.be/hnHki6AW0qY.

"'Zen Master' NBA Coach Phil Jackson Reveals His Secrets to Success." LAist - NPR News for Southern California - 89.3 FM, July 6, 2016. https://www.kpcc.org/show/airtalk/2014-01-01/zen-master-nba-coach-phil-jackson-reveals-his-secrets-to-success.

Ziglar, Zig, and Omar Akram. *Inspiration: 365 Days a Year*. Naperville, IL: Simple Truths, 2008.

For more great information, please visit:

thefinancialflow.com

There, you can sign up for my newsletter,
join my podcast, "Finding Financial Flow,"
and access free content designed to inform and inspire you.

Made in USA - North Chelmsford, MA
50142_9798392299430
12.26.2023 2219